THE STRUGGLE TO BE STRONG

UPDATED EDITION

True Stories by Teens About Overcoming Tough Times

Edited by
Al Desetta, M.A., for Youth Communication
and Sybil Wolin, Ph.D.

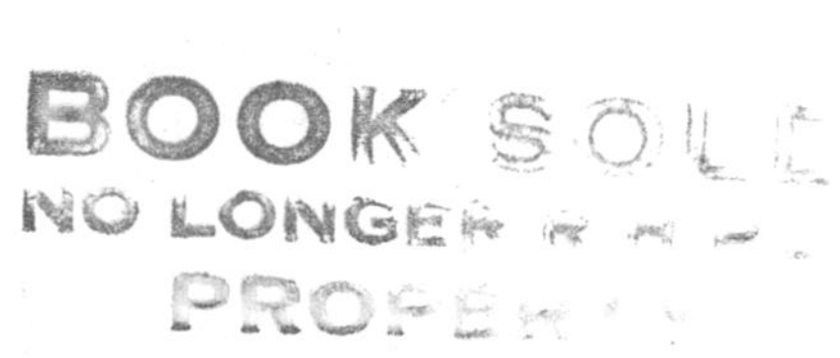

free spirit
PUBLISHING®

Library of Congress Cataloging-in-Publication Data
Names: Desetta, Al, editor. | Wolin, Sybil, editor.
Title: The struggle to be strong : true stories by teens about overcoming tough times / edited by Al Desetta, M.A., for Youth Communication, Sybil Wolin, Ph.D.
Description: Updated Edition. | Minneapolis : Free Spirit Publishing Inc., [2019] | Revised edition of The struggle to be strong, 2000. | Audience: Ages 13+
Identifiers: LCCN 2019013641 (print) | LCCN 2019980440 (ebook) | ISBN 9781631984617 (pdf) | ISBN 9781631984600 (paperback) | ISBN 9781631984624 (epub) | ISBN 1631984608 (paperback) | ISBN 9781631984600(paperback) | ISBN 1631984608(paperback) | ISBN 9781631984624(epub) | ISBN 9781631984617(pdf)
Subjects: LCSH: Teenagers—United States—Social conditions—Case studies—Juvenile literature. | Resilience (Personality trait) in adolescence—Case studies—Juvenile literature. | Teenagers—United States—Conduct of life—Juvenile literature. | Teenagers—United States—Biography—Juvenile literature.
Classification: LCC HQ796 (ebook) | LCC HQ796 .S874 2019 (print) | DDC 305.2350973—dc23
LC record available at https://lccn.loc.gov/2019013641

In the following stories, some names and/or identifying details have been changed: "I'm Black, He's Puerto Rican . . . So What?," "Not a Girl at All," "She's My Sister (Not Foster)," "Walking Out the Anger," "No One Spoke Up for Irma," and "I Was a Cyberbully."

The quotation on page 91 is from *101 Ways to Flirt: How to Get More Dates and Meet Your Mate* by Susan Rabin and Barbara Lagowski (New York: Plume, 1997).

Reading Level High School–Adult; Interest Level Ages 13 & Up;
Fountas & Pinnell Guided Reading Level Z+

Cover and interior design: Shannon Pourciau
Freelance editor: Bonnie Z. Goldsmith

10 9 8 7 6 5 4 3 2 1
Printed in the United States of America
V20300719

Free Spirit Publishing Inc.
6325 Sandburg Road, Suite 100
Minneapolis, MN 55427-3674
(612) 338-2068
help4kids@freespirit.com
freespirit.com

To the teens at Youth Communication, who have courageously shared their stories of persistence in the face of adversity.

ACKNOWLEDGMENTS

This book would not exist without the hard work, talent, and courage of the young writers whose stories give it life. They are part of a much larger group of young people at Youth Communication who have written about their lives since 1980. While we were able to include only thirty of the more than one hundred stories we considered for this book, we are moved and inspired by all of them.

From Al Desetta: I would like to thank Leah Weinman for her many insightful contributions to this project.

From Sybil Wolin: I would like to thank my husband, Steven Wolin, for daring to suggest that we write a book together and for his devotion during our work as coauthors. *The Resilient Self*, published by Villard Press in 1993, was the successful outcome of his suggestion. It is the source of the seven resiliencies that serve as the organizing principle of *The Struggle to Be Strong*.

I also would like to thank my granddaughter, Zoe, whose strength inspires me and affirms my commitment to the concept of psychological resilience.

We would like to thank Keith Hefner, cofounder and executive director of Youth Communication, for his support, guidance, and ideas.

Many foundations, corporations, and others support Youth Communication's work to train teens to tell their stories. One anonymous donor in particular has supported our work to promote resilience. We deeply appreciate her support and insight.

The work that created *The Struggle to Be Strong* was also supported by the Child Welfare Fund, the DeWitt-Wallace Reader's Digest Foundation, JP Morgan, the New York Community Trust, the New York Foundation, the Pinkerton Foundation, the Scherman Foundation, the WKBJ Partnership Foundation, the Ackman Family Fund, the Altman Foundation, the Annie Casey Foundation, the Stella and Charles Guttmann Foundation, the Bay Foundation, Bertelsman Music Group, the Booth Ferris Foundation, the Boyd Foundation, the Catalog for Giving, the Charles Hayden Foundation, Chase Manhattan Bank, Citibank, the Colin Higgins Foundation, Dress Barn, the Fund for the City of New York, the Yip Harburg Foundation, the Heckscher Foundation for Children, the Henry van Ameringen Foundation, the Kenworthy-Swift Foundation, Keyspan Energy, the Joseph E. Seagram and Sons, Inc. Fund, the Merchants & Traders Bank, Manhattan Borough Presidents Ruth Messinger and Virginia Fields, the Metzger-Price Fund, Morgan Stanley, the Samuel I. Newhouse Foundation, the City of New York's Department of Youth & Community Development, the New York Times Company Foundation, the Open Society Institute, the Paul Rapoport Foundation, the Public Welfare Foundation, the Rita and Stanley Kaplan Foundation, former New York State Senator Tom Duane, Time Warner, and the Valentine Perry Snyder Fund.

Several people read the manuscript and made important contributions: Chris Henrikson at the Dreamyard Drama Project in Los Angeles; Anthony Conelli, former director of Forsyth Satellite High School in New York and currently chair of the leadership department at the Bank Street Graduate School of Education; high school teacher Alison Koffler; and Tom Brown, the administrative director at Youth Communication.

We would like to thank the Youth Communication editors who worked with several of the writers on their stories: Susie Armitage, Rachel Blustain, Andrea Estepa, Philip Kay, Nora McCarthy, and Virginia Vitzthum. Youth Communication teen writers Cheryl Davis and Phillip Hodge gave many helpful comments on the manuscript.

Finally, we would like to thank freelance editor Bonnie Goldsmith, who edited *The Struggle to Be Strong*, and our team at Free Spirit: Judy Galbraith and Marjorie Lisovskis for their editorial guidance and support and longstanding interest in this project and Cassie Labriola-Sitzman for treating editing as a matter of offering suggestions, for following every suggestion by asking "Do you agree?" and for continuing to propose alternatives until the answer was "Yes."

CONTENTS

A MESSAGE TO YOU

"THINGS WILL GET BETTER."

I remember my guidance counselor telling me that while I was in his office. I had just gotten into a fight in the schoolyard with this kid who thought it was a good idea to smack me in the head and run away. (Ha! I showed him.) I was about to get suspended. I thought to myself, "Things will get better? Yeah, right."

After school, that same kid was waiting for me with a bunch of his friends. They beat me bloody, and no one tried to stop them. "Things will never get better," I thought to myself.

But you know what? Things always get better. Maybe not today, tomorrow, or even the next day, but they will, and that's what resilience is all about—regaining self. If I told you half the things I was able to bounce back from, you'd be mortified. You might even reexamine your own problems and decide they're not as bad as you thought. I hope the stories in *The Struggle to Be Strong* help you realize that there's always a way out of "no way out."

LENNY JONES*

*Lenny wrote the story "My Hair Is Blue—But I'm Not a Freak!" in this book. See page 126.

INTRODUCTION

A WAY OUT OF "NO WAY OUT"

by Veronica Chambers

Where does it come from—the ability to be strong? How do you struggle to survive when it feels like you've been born in the wrong skin, the wrong body, the wrong family, the wrong neighborhood, or on the wrong side of the tracks? How do you make your way when grown-ups who are supposed to take care of you fail miserably at their jobs? How do you try to move forward with your life when your parents, friends, or the kids at school don't know where you're coming from or what you have to deal with every day?

The teenage authors of *The Struggle to Be Strong* don't have all the answers, but they do a hell of a job wrestling with the questions. The wisdom they've gained is what makes this book so powerful, and what can help you face tough issues as you move toward adulthood. These thirty stories offer many lessons learned, from Youniqiue Symone's painful reckoning with her drug-addicted mother in "I Don't Know What the Word *Mommy* Means" to Artiqua S. Steed's exploration of interracial dating in "I'm Black, He's Puerto Rican . . . So What?" to Tamara Ballard's story of becoming tight with a girl she never thought she'd be proud to call sister in "She's My Sister (Not Foster)."

These stories first appeared in two youth magazines in New York City called *New Youth Connections* and *Foster Care Youth United* (now known as ***YC****teen* and *Represent*, respectively) and were originally published together in the first edition of *The Struggle to Be Strong* in 2000. The young writers wrote their stories to help teens like you with similar problems and stresses. And their stories continue to provide advice, inspiration, and hope. No matter what your life is like, the stories in this updated edition of *The Struggle to Be Strong* can help you realize your own strengths so you can face the future with greater confidence.

As you read these stories, don't think these kids are different from you—that because they're published in a book, they're somehow more special or together than you are. They've dealt with many of the same difficulties and challenges you've dealt with, and there's no shame in having problems. When you find ways to struggle through your challenges, you're already more remarkable than you may realize. The very things that seem to be ruining your life right now—having trouble controlling your anger, having an alcoholic parent, being too shy to make friends, living in a foster home—may be the very things that will give you the strength to face and deal with future obstacles as they come your way.

A person who keeps going despite hardships and setbacks, who learns positive, powerful lessons from these experiences, is a person with resilience. Resilience means inner strength. Since this is a book about resilience, in a way it's a book for everyone, because we all have the ability to bounce back from setbacks, disappointments, and loss. But this book will be especially valuable to young people who have had more than their share of troubles.

I know, because when I was sixteen, it seemed like there was nowhere for me to go but straight down the gutter. I had moved out of my mother's house because I didn't get along with my stepfather. Then when I moved in with my father and stepmother, the abuse just hit a whole new level. I spent many nights at the homes of friends, working in restaurants as a bus girl so I could get something to eat, or just walking the streets, hoping nobody would see me or hurt me.

I used to look at reruns of old TV shows like *The Brady Bunch* and think, "I bet every one of those cabinets in that TV kitchen has food in it. I bet those kids are never hungry." I liked school, but it's hard to study when you're afraid to go home. By the time my junior year rolled around, I was just trying to make it through each day. I had always dreamed of going to college, and I carefully avoided both sex and drugs because I didn't want an unplanned pregnancy or an addiction to derail me as they had some of my friends. But the question I had to wrestle with was: If I couldn't finish high school, if there was no safe place for me to live while I finished high school, how was I ever going to make it to college?

If you have a dream for your life, and if you try hard enough and you knock on enough doors, eventually you'll find what you need. With the help of my guidance counselor, Mrs. Chatmon, I applied to and was accepted at Simon's Rock, a college for kids who want to go to college early. I just knew that if I didn't find a way out of my situation, I wouldn't survive. My dream was to go to college, but the longer I stayed in my abusive household, the more I felt the dream slipping away from me.

So I went to college early, and it saved my life. Without really being fully aware of it, I was taking initiative, forming relationships, and trying to become independent. That's what the authors in this book, who are no different from you or me, have done in their lives. They haven't always succeeded and their problems haven't completely disappeared, but they have gained strength and grown through their efforts.

I once read something I've never forgotten. Angela Davis, scholar and activist, was talking about the Black Power movement of the 1960s. Here's the gist of what she said: "The thing we didn't understand back then is that freedom is an inside job."

I believe that with all my heart: "Freedom is an inside job." It may take you years to change your outside world and realize your dreams, but it's within your power to change your heart and mind. You might not think you have the power to change whatever in your life is causing you pain. But these teenage writers provide some valuable clues about how to begin tapping into that power.

Resilience isn't one specific magical quality that you're either born with or not. There are many kinds of resilience, and all of them can become part of you. This book is about seven kinds of resilience identified by Sybil Wolin, coeditor of *The Struggle to Be Strong*, and Steven Wolin. Together, the Wolins founded Project Resilience to conduct research and provide training in resilience. Learning about these resiliencies can help you think about ways you struggle to be strong. Each suggests actions you can take to survive, grow, and learn from the difficulties in your life. The seven resiliencies the Wolins identified are:

- Insight, or Asking Tough Questions
- Independence, or Being Your Own Person
- Relationships, or Connecting with People Who Matter
- Initiative, or Taking Charge

- Creativity, or Using Imagination
- Humor, or Finding What's Funny
- Morality, or Doing the Right Thing

You may feel you already have many of these resiliencies. Or you may feel you have none of them—or only one or two, in the tiniest portions.

Don't worry. It's not how often you act in these ways that counts—rather, it's your willingness to *build on what you've got*. You can learn to recognize what your strengths are and use them for all they're worth.

This book isn't called *Triumphant Stories of Teenagers with Unbelievable Will and Might*. It's called *The Struggle to Be Strong*, and the key word here is *struggle*. Struggle means making the effort to be strong. You have the power to "walk out" your anger, as Tamara Ballard did. You have the power to step in and be an example to your brothers and sisters when your parents are behaving irresponsibly, as Charlene Johnson did. You have the power to befriend someone living with AIDS, as Max Morán did.

If every day you do one little thing to make your life better, then guess what? You win. Because if you make that effort every day, your life will change. As teen writer Lenny Jones puts it, "If I told you half the things I was able to bounce back from, you'd be mortified." Still, Lenny insists, "But you know what? Things always get better."

That's what the stories in this book are about. By reading them, thinking about them, and trying to see how they relate to your life you can, as Lenny says, find "a way out of 'no way out.'"

VERONICA CHAMBERS is the editor of Past Tense, an archival storytelling project at the *New York Times*. She's the coauthor of four best-selling memoirs and the recipient of a James Beard award for her food writing. She's also the editor of the recent anthology *Queen Bey: A Celebration of the Power and Creativity of Beyoncé Knowles-Carter*.

You can follow Veronica on Twitter @vvchambers. She was in the Youth Communication writing program when she was an early college student at Bard College at Simon's Rock.

"THINK ABOUT IT"— AND MAYBE WRITE ABOUT IT

At the end of each story, you'll find a couple of questions under the heading "Think About It." These are to help you reflect on what you've read and find parallels between your experience and the writer's. Take a few moments to read them over. There's no need to write anything.

However, if you feel like it, jot down some of your thoughts. You don't have to write a lot—a few sentences can help you clarify your reactions to what you read.

Maybe you've had the experience of keeping a diary or journal, or writing letters or emails. If so, you know that writing helps you learn things about yourself and gives you a good way to deal with difficult emotions. Writing about your feelings can help you gain more control over them.

Terry-Ann Da Costa has written a story called "How Writing Helps Me," (page 112). Here's how she describes the importance of writing:

"I remember one day I was really depressed. I wrote about how I felt and what made me feel that way, and then I read over what I'd written. That helped me feel a lot better, because when I read it I couldn't believe I was capable of having those harmful, dangerous thoughts and feelings about myself.

"Writing helped me when I was going through difficult times with my family—when they didn't or couldn't understand me, or when they didn't understand why I would cry for no reason. Writing helped me when I needed someone to talk to. Writing is like both my friend and my family, because it's always there for me whenever I need it."

Lenny Jones, author of "My Hair Is Blue—But I'm Not a Freak!" (page 126), has this to say about writing:

"I realized there was always something going on in my life that I could write about from my own point of view. I could tell the stories I wanted to tell, and no one could tell me if I was right or wrong. I started to see writing as a really fun way of expressing myself and what I felt inside."

You certainly don't need to write answers to the questions under "Think About It." Just thinking about the questions is enough. But if you feel the urge to do so, writing your responses may deepen your enjoyment and understanding of this book.

NOTE: Many stories in *The Struggle to Be Strong* include slang or possibly unfamiliar words. The glossary on page 171 provides definitions of some of these words.

Each story ends with information about where each author was shortly after the events of the story. In some cases, we've lost contact with the writers. When possible, however, we've briefly described on page 169 where authors are now and what they are doing.

THE RESILIENCIES

INSIGHT

ASKING TOUGH QUESTIONS

INSIGHT is asking tough questions and giving honest answers about yourself and the difficult situations you find yourself in.

The opposite of **INSIGHT** is avoiding a painful truth.

INSIGHT is hard because the urge to blame others for your troubles, instead of looking honestly at your own role, is powerful.

INSIGHT helps you see things as they really are, not as you wish they would be.

Insight, our first resilience, is the habit of asking tough questions—about yourself and about the situations you find yourself in—and giving honest answers. With insight, you can face a painful truth instead of avoiding it. Insight is a resilience because it helps you open your eyes to situations as they really are, not as you wish they were.

The stories in this section are by teens who have struggled with difficult truths about themselves, their families, and their communities. You'll see them examine their own actions, face problems, and risk being hurt. As you may know from your own experience, it's often easier to ignore or deny what you don't like about yourself or your life than it is to face your problems squarely.

Having insight means you don't blame others for your problems. You take responsibility for yourself. It takes work—and courage—to face the truth this way. But insight helps the teens in this section become the people they really want to be. Insight can do the same for you.

I DON'T KNOW WHAT THE WORD *MOMMY* MEANS

by Younigiue Symone

If you looked at any of my baby pictures, you would see a little girl who seemed happy, loved, and cared for. You'd think this little girl would never go through any pain. You would probably also think that her mother was a proud and strong Hispanic woman who took care of her three daughters.

But the hardcore truth is, my mother didn't take care of us. She couldn't cope with herself, let alone three daughters. For a while, when people asked me why I lived with my aunt, I would say my mother died when I was three. But the truth is, she left me and my sisters and gave us to my aunt to raise.

When I was four, I used to watch TV and see mothers tuck their children in or read them a bedtime story. I asked my aunt and uncle why they never did these things. They told me only white people did them. Then one day I told my uncle that my friend's mother tucked her in and read her a story. He told me, "Your friend's mother is trying to be white."

For a long time my aunt and uncle would hide behind the excuse of "acting white" because they didn't want to show me any affection. For a long time I wanted to be white, because for everything I saw and asked about, I always got the same answer—they were either white or trying to be white. I used to listen to rock and roll, and when I was younger I couldn't really dance that well. My family used to make fun of me and call me "white girl." That was just another example of how my aunt and uncle never showed me love.

> **"But the hardcore truth is, my mother didn't take care of us. She couldn't cope with herself, let alone three daughters."**

When I was four I started to rebel against my mother. I always was a child who would look at a problem—and not only look at it but also speak out on it, instead of trying to ignore it. My sisters used to say, "When I see Mommy, I'm gonna tell her to get herself together." But when Mommy came around to visit at my aunt's, they would forget all about it.

My sisters would tell our mother how much they missed her or how they loved her. Instead, I'd say to her, "I wish you would get yourself together. I wish you would stop using drugs." My mother just told me my mouth would get me in trouble. She told me that a lot of times, or she'd say that I kept bringing up stuff instead of just letting it be. I had to teach myself not to settle for less. My family hated the fact that I spoke out.

They hated the fact that I knew what was going on and that I always questioned things when no one else did. For example, I also asked my mother, "How come you had us when you weren't going to take care of us?" My mother would just look at me, cry, and walk away, or she'd say as always, "Your mouth is going to get you in trouble."

> **"I had to teach myself not to settle for less. My family hated the fact that I spoke out."**

I hated when my mother came around, period. It wasn't bad enough that we didn't live with her or that she knew we were getting abused but didn't do anything to help us. She acted like her life was more important than ours. Gradually, I wished she wasn't my mother, and she wished I wasn't her child.

My mother had a rough childhood. Her own mother would rather gamble than put food on the table. And my grandmother's mother gave my grandmother up. So really, no one in my family had a good mother or was a good mother. They all wanted to show their mothers how to be mothers by having children at a young age.

But having children that way doesn't make you a mother. I believe my mother had me and my sisters young to show my grandparents what a "real family" could be. I also believe she wanted a family so badly that sometimes she would push us too hard and sometimes she didn't push us enough.

For example, my mother always used to tell us that she was trying to get herself together. But she didn't push herself enough to give up drugs, because her will wasn't strong enough. When my mother finally did come around to see us, she wanted our relationship to be so perfect. She wanted me to tell her everything. She wanted to make up in two hours for all the time she missed. She pushed me too hard. She wanted to bring us together so fast that instead she pushed us apart.

To this day we still don't get along. I feel if she wanted to live her life, she didn't have to bring me and my sisters into this world. I always used to dream about her coming to get us and taking us away. We would live in a house and she would have a job. I dreamed we would just be one big, happy family, but finally I can say I grew up.

I grew up when I realized this: My mother is not going to change because I want her to. She's only going to change when she wants to. I also know, deep down in my heart, that we are never going to be a real family. As long as she tries to tell me what to do, I'm going to rebel, and as long as I tell her what to do, she's going to rebel.

Our relationship is no relationship at all. We don't have any communication whatsoever. My mother is now married and says she is living her life for her husband. If my mother doesn't want anything to do with me or my sisters, that's her loss, not ours! Today I am in school (with no children, thank God), and I have a life. Before I have any children, I am going to take parenting skills classes. I won't hurt my children the way I was hurt.

"I want to break the cycle."

I don't want to have children at a young age to show my mother what a "real mother" is. I want to break the cycle. If I don't, I might end up doing the same thing my mother did. I might hurt not only myself or my family, but everyone else I come in contact with.

YOUNIQIUE SYMONE was sixteen and living in foster care when she wrote this story. She eventually returned to her family.

THINK ABOUT IT

- Think of a time when you were at odds with a family member or friend because of a problem that no one wanted to talk about or confront. Did you speak out? What happened when you did? If you didn't speak out, how did it feel to keep silent?
- What is a "cycle" in your own life you'd like to break? How could you go about breaking it?

BEAUTY IS MORE THAN SKIN DEEP

by Danielle Wilson

My friends always ask me, "Why are you always looking in the mirror?" or "Why are you so confident about yourself?" I know it might be hard to believe, but until the age of fourteen, I never really thought of myself as beautiful or gorgeous or ugly. I thought of myself as an average person.

When I was twelve, I didn't really care how I looked. I was a short, skinny girl with a couple of ponytails (because my grandmother used to do my hair all the time) and thousands of bumps on my face.

In my sixth-grade class, this boy used to call me "Bumpy Road" or "Mountain." Yeah, it used to get to me. In fact, it got to me so much that I knocked him right out of his chair. I know that was mean, but he was being mean to me!

And guess what? He saw me recently, and he now wants to know when I'm going to be his girl. Please! I wouldn't give him the time of day because he hasn't changed. But I certainly have.

> "I became stuck-up because I was getting compliments like crazy and I wasn't used to this kind of attention."

During the summer when I turned fourteen, I began recognizing my beauty a little more. I started by taking care of my face. Not only by washing it fifty times a day, but also by cutting back on chocolate and going to the skin doctor for my acne.

Of course, boys started to notice me. I've always had a perfect shape and never had a problem with my weight. I also changed the way I dressed. I started to show off my figure by wearing skirts and jeans that really fit.

I started doing my own hair too. I can't really remember how I did it, but my grandmother used to say, "Girl, you come up with the weirdest hairstyles. Just like your mother when she was little."

That was the best summer of my life because I was getting mad compliments from the cutest boys. Whenever they complimented me I used to say, "I know!" because I knew I looked good. Didn't I?

I became stuck-up because I was getting compliments like crazy and I wasn't used to this kind of attention. Before I turned fourteen, I don't think anybody ever noticed me. Now that I had blossomed like a flower, I wanted the whole world to know. You can say I got a big head because every time I passed a car window, I stared at my reflection and sang to myself that I was the most beautiful thing in the world.

When I was younger, I never looked in mirrors because I didn't like what I saw. Meaning, a face full of pimples. Now mirrors became my life. Before, I never liked having my picture taken. I used to try to hide in the back, but my friends always wanted me in the front because I was the smallest. Now I began to love having people take pictures of me.

"Now that I had blossomed like a flower, I wanted the whole world to know."

It got so bad that my attitude got worse, but only toward boys. I used to tell them, "I'm too pretty to be with you."

I remember one day (about two years ago) I went with my friend to her boyfriend's house. There was a boy there who wanted to meet me, and he was not what I expected. In fact, I thought he was ugly. He had little beady eyes and BIG lips. He sort of scared me!

The first time I looked at him, I yelled "No!" really loud. Then I turned to my friend and yelled, "He is *so* ugly. What's wrong with you? Why did you try to play me and hook me up with this thing?" I thought I looked so good I couldn't stand to be around anyone ugly.

After he heard that, he left. I guess he was mad. Then my friend's boyfriend said I was wrong. I said, "I can't help it if your friend is ugly. You know, you shouldn't hang out with ugly people because they make you look bad." After that, a friend picked me up and I left.

Another time, a boy tried to talk to me when my friends and I were coming from a party. And I ran from him because I didn't like the shape of his head. His head was little on a big body. He looked like a cartoon, and he had scars and pimples all over his face!

My friends never forgot that. They tease me about it to this day.

I used to tell boys to their faces that they were ugly and that I looked too good to be with them. And they would just stand there and take what I said. None of them ever cursed me out or raised their hands to me. But then one day, when I was about fifteen, a boy named Rick turned my whole attitude around.

"I started to realize I had let my looks take over my inner person."

Rick and I were sitting in the park, and we were arguing. He never was my man, but we were friends leading to that. We had met at a party, but his friend liked me. I got mad at something I can't quite remember, and I said to Rick, "I'm too pretty to be with you or your friend."

Rick said, "You're right, but with that attitude you'll be by yourself. You could be as pretty as you wanna be to boys, but if you have a bad attitude, they won't want anything to do with you. They will do nothing but use you." And then he walked away.

Right then and there I wanted to run up to him and curse him out because I couldn't believe what he had said to me. I was furious! I was so furious that I wanted to call him later to curse him out. But when I got home, I was too mad to do it. And besides, I knew he was going to call me to apologize. But I was wrong. Rick never called.

I thought about what Rick said and about all the times I told boys I was too pretty for them. I started to realize I had let my looks take over my inner person. I didn't even remember how I used to be. My stuck-up attitude had become my whole personality. And I told myself I was going to change. Changing wasn't easy, because there were still times when I wanted to tell a boy I was too pretty for him, but I made myself hold back.

The reason why Rick had such a big impact on me was because he was the first and only boy who wouldn't let me talk to him like that. He stood up to me, and I'm glad he did before my attitude got worse.

For a while I lost my friendship with Rick. A little later on down the line we started being friends again, but we never discussed what had happened between us.

Even now I still look in the mirror for hours and I look into car windows, checking out my reflection. There's nothing wrong with that. You don't have to be stuck-up just because you admire yourself.

But after Rick said that to me, I started to be nice to boys. I accepted compliments in a nicer way by saying "Thank you" every time someone said I was pretty, instead of "I know."

I also started paying more attention to my interests, like writing and reading. I wrote short stories for contests in my school, and once I won second place. As I improved my writing, I finally won first place. I was so happy!

"What I learned was this: To be beautiful outside, you have to be beautiful inside too."

I never really thought I was such a creative writer until I wrote a story in my eighth-grade class and let my friend Jody read it. Jody loved it so much she showed it to my classmates and then to my teacher, who put it in the school newspaper.

I did more than help myself. I helped someone else—my friend Tasha.

Tasha wasn't stuck-up like me. She was miserable all the time because she thought she was ugly. Tasha used to ask me, "How do you get your hair like that?" So one day I told her I was going to do her hair.

After I did her hair, she was still a little doubtful about her looks because she didn't like the way she dressed. So I took Tasha shopping. (Not with *my* money, with *her* money. I didn't become *that* nice.) And we had a blast.

I didn't tell her what to pick out. It was her choice. But she asked me for advice and fashion tips. After we finished, Tasha said she felt great and that she'd never had so much fun in her life. She also said she owed it all to me. Then I told her, "It wasn't me who changed you, *you* changed you. Now, don't change your attitude because you changed your looks. Stay the nice person you are."

If it weren't for Rick, I wouldn't have done this for Tasha. I probably would have thought Tasha just wanted to be like me or something. What I learned was this: To be beautiful outside, you have to be beautiful inside too.

So, if you're someone like me, take my advice: Looks ain't everything! I had to learn the hard way. But if you're someone who isn't hung up on your looks—don't change your attitude.

DANIELLE WILSON was sixteen when she wrote this story. She later graduated from high school.

THINK ABOUT IT

- Think of a time when someone told you something about yourself that was true, but that you didn't want to hear. Did you get angry and dismiss what you were told? Or did you listen and take steps to change? Why was it difficult to hear what the person had to say?
- What is a difficult truth about yourself that you've resisted seeing? Why do you think you've resisted seeing it?

CONTROLLING MY TEMPER

by Christopher A. Bogle

When I got back to my group home one Friday night, a staff member named Robert was giving out the allowances. Ms. Torres, the supervisor of the group home, usually makes out the allowance sheet, but that Friday she wasn't there because of some family difficulties.

Ms. Torres is a fair person who had always given me what I deserved. Since she wasn't there, I was worried I wasn't going to get the right amount of allowance for the chores I'd completed. Other staff members sometimes gave the residents less than they deserved. That week I'd completed over twenty chores, and each chore was worth two dollars.

> **"My mother had always told me not to let anybody put their hands on me."**

As I expected, Robert didn't know what he was doing. He said each chore was worth $1.20. When I signed for my allowance, I was ticked off because I was being jerked. When I tried to explain to Robert that I deserved more money, he kept on making excuses. I was getting even more mad, because I felt he wasn't taking me seriously.

I was trying to save so I could buy a jacket for the winter. I was short five dollars. I needed a jacket badly, because the one I had didn't keep me warm. I'd decided to cash in a savings bond I had won in a spelling bee so I could buy the jacket. When I asked Robert for the savings bond, he refused to give it to me. He thought it was in my best interest to save it for my college education.

I kept on repeating that I wanted to cash in the savings bond, but Robert still refused to give it to me. The bond was in my folder in the filing cabinet where the staff kept the important papers.

I was so mad that I put my arm in the filing cabinet when Robert opened it. When I refused to remove my arm, he closed the drawer on my hand and hurt me. He told me to get out of the office, but I refused.

Then Robert grabbed me and tried to push me out of the office. I was ready to swing at him. My mother had always told me not to let anybody put their hands on me. But I knew if I hit

Robert, I would probably get arrested for assaulting him. The police would never believe it was self-defense.

The supervisor on duty had gone out of the house while this incident was taking place. When he came back and heard me using profanity at Robert, he tried to calm me down. When I explained what had happened, the supervisor told me to keep my head and said he'd take care of the problem. I maintained my temper and just chilled.

When the supervisor came out of the office, he gave me my savings bond and explained that the situation had been taken care of. But in my mind the situation was not resolved because I felt I was the victim of wrongful doing.

"You can solve problems without using violence. You have to be smart and willing to work things out."

That same night my cousin Eric called me. Eric always looked out for me. When I explained to him what had happened, he got so mad he was about to jump in his car and drive down to see Robert. I told him not to come down because Robert had gone off duty at six and he'd be wasting his time.

When Eric came to the group home a few weeks later to drive me home for Christmas vacation, he wanted to see Robert. I tried to convince him to forget about it, but my cousin still wanted to see him.

Robert was in the office talking on the phone. Eric walked in and introduced himself, and Robert did the same. My cousin started asking him about how the problem started.

Robert closed the office door. I got scared because I didn't want to see my cousin get himself in trouble. I was scared Eric would punch Robert in the face. I knew my cousin sometimes had a temper. I listened at the door. I was relieved when I heard them talking, not fighting.

When Eric came out of the office, he said good-bye to Robert and we left.

When we got in the car, Eric told me everything was taken care of. He'd told Robert never to put his hands on me again, and that if he had a problem with me to call him and he would take care of everything.

I had gotten very angry when Robert refused to give me my savings bond, but I should have handled myself better. I knew Ms. Torres was coming in on Sunday. I should have been patient and waited for her to handle the dispute. If I had to do it over, I would never have gone inside the office and been disrespectful to Robert.

But I also feel Robert was more at fault than I was. He tried to hurt me by closing the file cabinet on my hand. Robert is a staff member and I'm a minor in foster care. He should have handled the situation in a better way by calling Ms. Torres and asking her if he should give me my savings bond. Looking back, in a way I'm sorry I cashed it, but it was also my right to cash it if I wanted to.

The way my cousin Eric handled the situation had a very big impact on me. When I used to get mad, I never talked about my problem with the person I was mad at. I held it inside until I exploded. Hearing how my cousin talked it out with Robert showed me how to express myself better and say what's on my mind.

> "When I get mad now, I isolate myself from everybody until I calm down."

You can solve problems without using violence. You have to be smart and willing to work things out. The first thing I will try in the future is to talk.

I still get angry, but since the incident with Robert I have calmed down a little. I don't get mad as fast as I used to. I still have a problem controlling my temper, but I try my best to avoid a situation when I know I'm going to get mad.

To anybody who ends up in a situation like this, please think before you react. You might do something you will later regret. If you do get mad, talk to someone. Also, get out of the house and go for a walk. When I get mad now, I isolate myself from everybody until I calm down.

CHRISTOPHER A. BOGLE was seventeen when he wrote this story. Later, he attended Long Island University for two years as a political science/sociology major. He then went on to graduate from Marine Corps basic training. Christopher is also the author of "Learning to Forgive" (page 81).

For more about where Christopher is now, see page 169.

THINK ABOUT IT

- Have you ever been treated unfairly by someone who had power over you? What happened? How did you deal with your feelings?
- Think of a way you sometimes react under stress that can have a negative result. What new kind of behavior would be more productive? Why?

THE ANSWER WAS ME

by Eliott Castro

About a year ago I thought I was losing my mind. The girl I loved decided to break up with me. Today I don't blame her for leaving me, but at the time, losing her hurt me a lot.

She broke up with me because I had a drinking problem she knew nothing about when she first met me, but which got worse during our relationship.

At the time, I was living with my mother. I was being faced with verbal and sometimes physical abuse from her. I tried to bottle up my feelings by drowning them in alcohol. But this did no good, because I started verbally abusing my girlfriend, taking out on her the frustration and anger that my mother caused me.

> "Hiding from a problem is never the way to go about resolving it, no matter how harsh the problem might be or how hard it is to face it."

Eventually we broke up, giving me a perfect opportunity to continue my drinking. From that point on I just went crazy. I was completely self-destructive every time I drank. I'd end up kicking and punching through glass or walls until my fists would bleed. Then I would drink some more to forget whatever embarrassing stunt I had pulled in the last few minutes.

I was going through so much pain and hurt that hiding from my problems in alcohol only made them worse. Hiding from a problem is never the way to go about resolving it, no matter how harsh the problem might be or how hard it is to face it.

Everyone goes through problems and everyone has different ways of dealing with them—reading a book, lifting weights, watching TV, or staying away from others. Now, what if I told you that these activities may not be the proper way of dealing with your problems? That watching TV or lifting weights can be as bad as drinking?

I'm saying this because people often avoid a problem by doing something they enjoy or that relaxes them so that they can get their mind off what's bothering them. I know, because that's exactly what I was doing. When I sobered up, the problem was right there waiting for me. The fact that I was no longer with my girl only hurt more because I didn't want to deal with it.

The same thing applies when you pick up a book or go watch TV. When you're done keeping yourself occupied, the problem is still going to be there, unless you decide to face it.

It isn't easy to admit to yourself or to anyone else that you have a problem, but it's necessary to do so in order to deal with it. Accepting the problem means looking at the trouble it is causing you and asking yourself: What can I do to solve this problem?

"Why was everything around me falling apart? What made me lose everything? Who was causing all this to happen? The only answer I could come up with was 'me.'"

I had to start somewhere, so I began at home. I had no choice but to leave my mother. She was keeping me from reaching my goal of getting on with my life.

Now that I was completely alone, it was easier to go anywhere I chose. I stumbled upon a nearby park that faces a river, and there I started to evaluate myself. I chose this park because of its beauty.

The setting was quiet, there weren't many people there, and in front of me were the river and the setting sun, which left a reflection of bright-colored lights on the water. Being there made it easier for me to look at myself and try to understand what I was doing wrong.

As the park relaxed my nerves, I started to look back on my life. Why was everything around me falling apart? What made me lose everything? Who was causing all this to happen?

The only answer I could come up with was "me." I realized that I had to make changes in my attitude and behavior. There was no one else to blame.

I evaluated why I needed to drink, why I was hurting, and what I was going to do to change things. I realized that I drank because I felt sorry for myself and because I didn't really want to know what I was feeling sorry about.

The "why" was that I loved my girlfriend and losing her was too painful to face. It hurt to think I once had someone so good, but lost her. What really made it painful was that I also drank so I could visualize her beside me. You might say I drank just to be with her again, to see her sitting down next to me.

I also realized that now I was putting the weight of my problems totally on my own shoulders. Which is why I had to take the next step.

That next step was hard. I realized that until I forgave myself, my problems wouldn't go away. I forgave myself for allowing the drinking to take over my life. I forgave myself for losing the girl I loved. I forgave myself for the physical and mental damage I had caused myself and others.

If I hadn't forgiven myself, I would have continued acting reckless. That was what I learned by sitting down and focusing my mind on solving my problems and not avoiding them.

Whatever it is you're going through, don't avoid your problems without getting some answers. Don't hide what you're going through—face it and make a change for the better.

"That next step was hard. I realized that until I forgave myself, my problems wouldn't go away."

Today I can deal with my problems and actually get things done by focusing on what I have to do. Of course, now and then I run into a little trouble, but I can handle it maturely. I don't hold anything back by feeling sorry for myself.

Some of my thanks go to that park by the river, but most of the credit goes to me.

ELIOTT CASTRO was eighteen when he wrote this story. He has lived in several group homes and shelters for homeless teens.

THINK ABOUT IT

- Insight—seeing things as they are—can be the first step in fighting an addiction like alcoholism. Think of a problem *you're* going through. What has helped you face it? If you haven't been able to face it, what has stood in the way?
- What is a favorite place you like to visit, a place that calms you and allows you to think clearly? What makes the place special?

COLOR ME DIFFERENT

by Jamal K. Greene

I am black. Yet, since I was twelve, I've gone to a school that has almost no black people. I don't speak in slang. I don't listen to rap or reggae, and try as I might, I have at best a fifty-fifty chance of converting a layup when I play basketball. Except for the fact that I'm not white, I'm not all that different from a stereotypical white kid from the suburbs.

Because of this, when I'm around other black people, I usually feel a certain distance between us. And so do they. For example, this past summer I took a journalism workshop at a local university. After it was over, I was on the phone with one of the girls in the workshop, a black girl, and we got to talking about first impressions. She said that for about the first week of the workshop, she was saying to herself, "What's wrong with this guy? Is he white or something?" She said I talked like a "cracker" (as she put it), and she made a lot of remarks about me not being a "real" black person. It irritated me that this girl thought just because I didn't speak black English, I was not a genuine black person.

"It irritated me that this girl thought just because I didn't speak black English, I was not a genuine black person."

I have often heard people criticize baseball announcer Paul Olden for the same thing. Olden is black, but you would never know it from the way he talks. They say he's trying to be white. I don't "sound black" either, and I'm not trying to be anything but who I am. It's just the way I talk. Black people who speak standard English don't do it because they want to distance themselves from other black people but because they grew up hearing English spoken that way.

Just look at former English boxer Lennox Lewis. He's black, but his accent is as British as can be. Is he "trying to be English" and denying his black roots? Of course not. He just grew up around people who had British accents.

I don't dance like a lot of other black people either. I never learned to move my hips and legs the way most kids you see at

"Contrary to popular belief, black people aren't born with the ability to dance and play basketball."

parties are able to. I lose the beat if I have to move more than two body parts at once, and so my dancing tends to get a little repetitive.

When I go to parties with black people, I often find myself sitting at the table drinking a soda while everybody else is dancing. "Why aren't you dancing?!" people ask. And then when I do get on the dance floor, the same people sneer at me. "What's wrong with you?" they say. "Why do you just keep doing the same thing over and over again?"

Contrary to popular belief, black people aren't born with the ability to dance and play basketball. Even though I have speed and leaping ability, I can't drive to the hole without losing my dribble. Those skills have to be learned and perfected with experience. It only seems like they're inborn because the black community in America is culturally very close-knit and people share the same interests.

Another thing that stands for "blackness" in a lot of people's minds is an interest in or a feeling of pride and identification with things historically black. I collected baseball cards until I was fifteen. I had a pretty substantial collection for a kid. At least I thought I did. One afternoon, my cousins came over to my house and were looking at my baseball cards.

"Do you have any Jackie Robinson cards?" one of them asked.

"Of course not," I answered.

They were not pleased with that response. Of course, in my mind I knew that the reason I didn't have any Jackie Robinson cards was the same reason I didn't have any Ted Williams or Mickey Mantle or Joe DiMaggio cards. I just didn't have the money for Jackie Robinson. Even if I were going to spend that much on baseball cards, I would buy a Mickey Mantle card before I would buy a Jackie Robinson card. Jackie may have been the first black major leaguer but Mickey hit home runs, and home runs increase in value faster than historical novelty. It's that simple. But my cousins thought the reason I didn't have any Jackie Robinson cards was because I didn't like black players as much as white players.

My family has always had a problem with me liking baseball—a game that did not integrate until 1947—as much as I do. They keep getting me these Negro League postcards because they're worried I don't know enough about the subject. And they're right. But then again, sports fans in general don't know enough about the Negro Leagues. My family feels very strongly that as a black sports fan, I should feel an added responsibility to know about black baseball players. If I don't learn about them, they say, then nobody will.

Minorities are often called upon to be the spokespeople for their races. The only black kid in the class is almost always asked to speak when the subjects of slavery or the civil rights movement come up. The question is, does the black kid have a responsibility to know more about issues relating to blacks than his white classmates do? I would like to think he doesn't.

"The question is, does the black kid have a responsibility to know more about issues relating to blacks than his white classmates do? I would like to think he doesn't."

If we really believe everyone should be treated equally, then my Jewish friends should be expected to know just as much about black history as I do. Of course I should know more about the Negro Leagues than I do now, but so should a white baseball fan or a Japanese baseball fan or a polka-dot baseball fan.

So I guess I don't fit in with the black people who speak black English, dance with a lot of hip motion, and hang out with an all-black crowd. And I don't feel any added responsibility to learn about black history or go out and associate with more black people either. Nor do I fit in with blacks like conservative Supreme Court Justice Clarence Thomas: To me it seems that they try as hard as they can to separate themselves from blacks altogether, vote Republican, and marry white women. I'm not like that either.

Even though I grew up playing Wiffle ball with white kids instead of basketball with black kids, even though I go to a school with very few blacks, and even though most of my friends are white and Asian, I can't say I feel completely at home with white people, either. Achieving racial equality is a process that still has a long way to go. Blacks were slaves less than 200 years ago. Until only a few decades ago, we were legally inferior to whites. Blacks may have achieved equality before the law, but it will take another few generations to achieve social equality.

There is still a lot of controversy attached to interracial relationships, for example, both romantic and otherwise. Whenever I'm around the parents of white friends, I get the sense that they see me not as "that nice kid who is friends with my son or daughter," but rather as "that nice *black* kid who is friends with my son or daughter." There is still a line certain people are unwilling to cross.

"I would like to think race is nothing more than the color of your skin."

So, after all this analysis, I'm still confused about what it means to be black. What is race anyway? According to *Merriam-Webster's Dictionary*, race is "a class or kind of people unified by shared interests, habits, or characteristics."

Well, anyone who's ever called me or any other black person "white on the inside" because we didn't fit their stereotype can look at that definition and claim victory. "There it is, right in the dictionary," they can say. "Black is an attitude, not just a color."

By that definition I'm not black at all. But I was black the last time I looked in the mirror. So I went back to the dictionary and found that *Merriam-Webster's* has another definition for race: "a category of humankind that shares certain distinctive physical traits." (In other words, race is based on one's *physical appearance*.)

Wait a minute! Does that mean that a black person is anyone with dark skin, full lips, a broad nose, and coarse hair? These are distinctive physical traits shared by black people. By the second definition, to be black means to have these physical characteristics. Speaking black English and dancing well are not genetic. They are cultural and arise from blacks living isolated from other communities.

Which definition is right? I would like to think it's the second. I would like to think race is nothing more than the color of your skin, but clearly in most people's minds it's more than that. I feel distanced from blacks because I'm black but don't act the part, and I feel distanced from whites because I act white but don't look the part. As long as people expect me to act a certain way because of the way I look or to look a certain way because of the way I act, I will continue to be something of an outcast because I defy their prejudices.

> "As long as people expect me to act a certain way because of the way I look or to look a certain way because of the way I act, I will continue to be something of an outcast because I defy their prejudices."

The reality is that I'm different from a stereotypical white kid from suburbia because, no matter how I act, others will see me differently. Society has different expectations for black and white people and becomes uncomfortable if we differ from those expectations. Just ask anybody who's ever picked me for a game of two-on-two basketball just because I was black.

JAMAL K. GREENE was seventeen when he wrote this story. He later graduated from Harvard College and became a reporter for *Sports Illustrated.*

For more about where Jamal is now, see page 169.

THINK ABOUT IT

- Have any people assumed something about you because of your race, gender, age, appearance, way of speaking, or any other reason? How hard was it for you to deal with their assumptions? Were they surprised when they found out more about you?
- Why do you think it's hard for people to accept behavior that's different from their own?

INDEPENDENCE

BEING YOUR OWN PERSON

INDEPENDENCE is being your own person and keeping an emotional distance between you and the pressures of family, friends, and circumstances.

The opposite of **INDEPENDENCE** is doing things only to get the approval of others or to avoid feeling alone or rejected.

INDEPENDENCE is hard because it sometimes means breaking or limiting connections with people who are important to you.

INDEPENDENCE helps you feel safe and know you can rely on yourself.

Independence, our second resilience, means being your own person. Sometimes that means stepping back from the pressures you feel from people and situations. You then can make conscious, thoughtful decisions about what you will and won't do. Independence requires that you look inward to see what's good and most important for you—and then look outward to see how you can get what you need. Independence is a resilience because it helps keep you focused on what *you* want out of life.

Becoming independent is hard work that never really ends. Sometimes you may make decisions you later regret because you want to be liked, or because it's easier to go along with family and friends. But independence helps you see more clearly what decisions are best for you.

You may know teens who are willing to take the risk of being independent. Independence sometimes seems like a leap into the dark. But by standing apart from the group and staying true to your personal values, you learn to make good decisions. You feel safe in knowing that you're not a pushover—you're an independent human being.

I WAS A BEAUTY SCHOOL SUCKER

by Tonya Leslie

A few years ago, as I was looking through a magazine, a headline loomed in my face: "Be a Model or Just Look Like One! Barbara's Beauty School Can Show You How."

I was ecstatic! How often had I dreamed of having my face on a magazine cover, of being sought after by the press and loved by the public? (So that's a little much, but you get the idea.)

Anyway, I begged the parents (that's what I call them) to let me go to Barbara's Beauty School. After all, how many times had I endured piano lessons and Girl Scouts—the things *they* wanted me to do? I had finally found something I wanted. The least they could do was finance it, right?

Right!

So we went for our initial visit to the local office. Upon looking at me, the woman in charge predicted my success as a model. They even sweet-talked my sister into joining as a kind of two-for-one deal.

After a few weeks of training, the woman said, my modeling success would be practically guaranteed. The parents, too, were so convinced that they didn't grumble about the $1,000-plus they kicked out. I guess they assumed we would make it all back.

"How often had I dreamed of having my face on a magazine cover, of being sought after by the press and loved by the public?"

At the first session, my sister and I were equipped with our modeling essentials: a handbook and a makeup brush kit. We had three hour-long classes every Saturday. They included makeup training, exercise class, and runway modeling.

The makeup classes were more like makeup disaster classes. Rather than telling us how to apply makeup according to our skin color (we're black) and the shape of our faces, they gave a general analysis. In other words, we all put on the same makeup, the same way.

What happened to the natural beauty of youth? Well, that's not the way at Barbara's Beauty School—they seemed to emphasize the more makeup, the better.

Fully loaded with makeup, we went on to runway modeling where we modeled imaginary clothing. You know, fur coats and other things we would never see. We were taught something called a model stance and shown how to go up and down steps.

Then we did group modeling, where we would pair off and make poses. I'd never seen runway shows like that, but I figured the teachers at Barbara's knew the deal better than I did. That was my first and constant mistake.

"After posing in a variety of outfits and makeup styles, I glanced in the mirror. My makeup and hair looked like something out of beauty school hell!"

Weeks passed and graduation approached. We grew bored with the classes so we skipped a few—well, more than a few. When we weren't really prepared for graduation, we decided to make up classes.

That was difficult because classes at Barbara's Beauty School go in no specific order. For example, on a Saturday you may take class number four without ever taking class number three. My sister and I ended up taking several classes over and over again. Not fun at all.

Finally, a year after we began, graduation was around the corner. A photographer was called in to take shots of the girls. This was to be very professional, so a makeup artist and hair stylist were called in too, although they were supposedly optional.

My sister and I wanted to do our own makeup and hair. We figured we knew what looked good, or at least we should after all this time and money. But my teacher assured me that their people were the very best. Then she commented that our hair and makeup hardly looked professional.

Recovering from that insult, we handed over the additional $35 each, figuring, once again, that the teachers knew best. Big mistake number two.

After posing in a variety of outfits and makeup styles, I glanced in the mirror. My makeup and hair looked like something out of beauty school hell!

First of all, my medium-toned skin, with the help of tons of foundation, was at least four tones darker. (Not to mention the lovely lines where my foundation and skin color didn't match.)

Then they showered me with frosted pink blush and lipstick, complete with baby-blue eye shadow. Those colors may work for Barbie, but not for me.

And then my hair. Let's just say that relaxed black hair should not be teased five feet and then sprayed with a can of hair spray. (Unless you like the tangled, dry, split-end—let's not forget flaky—look that will follow in the morning.)

"We felt bad because of the screaming fit the parents threw once they saw those ugly $300 pictures."

Upon viewing my stricken looks, the teacher told me that retouching and recoloring on photos is common (in my case, mandatory) and that the pictures would look great. Like a fool, I believed her, adding mistake number three. (Surely you're counting along, right?)

A couple of weeks later, the pictures were delivered to my house. Not only did we look bad (I would describe my sister's pictures, but she promised instant death at the mere mention), we felt bad.

Why, you ask?

We felt bad because of the screaming fit the parents threw once they saw those ugly $300 pictures.

Well, we didn't go to graduation after that little scene. In fact, we never went back. The pictures are still in the back of my sister's closet . . . somewhere. The parents make us take them out every once in a while—whenever I wonder aloud why they don't raise my allowance or why we never get gifts or have parties.

One day on the train, this guy approached me and said, "You look like a model." Then he handed me his card. I ripped it to pieces in his face.

I'm sure I don't have to tell you what company he was from.

TONYA LESLIE was eighteen when she wrote this story. She went on to earn a master's degree in education from New York University and became an editor for Scholastic Inc.

For more about where Tonya is now, see page 169.

THINK ABOUT IT

- Have you ever bought something that you thought would change you or your image? Did it? How?
- Think about a time you followed a dream that seemed realistic at the time but didn't turn out as you had hoped. How do you feel about that dream now?

MY WEIGHT IS NO BURDEN

by Charlene Johnson

A lot of people in this world want something so bad they're willing to do anything to get it. That's what happened to me. My desire was to be as thin as the models in fashion magazines. I wanted it so bad I almost killed myself.

I knew I wasn't the only teenage girl who felt this way. The media (magazines, movies, TV, and music) say that being thin is the way to be. I envied the slim models in their bikinis and tank tops, and I wanted to look just like them.

When I was between eleven and thirteen years old, I really didn't care too much about the way I looked. I always considered myself to be pleasingly plump. But when I started junior high school, I wanted to dress like a girl. Before that I always wore boys' clothes. I thought it was time for me to show my "feminine side."

"My desire was to be as thin as the models in fashion magazines. I wanted it so bad I almost killed myself."

One day I decided to go shopping for some school clothes. When I went to try on stuff, I had a little trouble fitting into the clothes I wanted. Even so, I bought them. I thought, "I am going on a diet." But that never happened. I ended up giving my sister all the clothes.

Soon my weight started to bother me so much that I began to throw up my food on purpose after a meal. This went on for several weeks. I stopped because it hurt my throat.

Then I began to eat very small portions of food. I felt sick some days and had a lot of headaches. I knew I had to go back to eating regularly. But after all that vomiting and eating like a four-year-old, I began to like the way my body was improving.

When I lost almost twenty pounds in a few weeks, I thought to myself, "Hey, why not have a nice snack?" That's where I went wrong. As soon as I started munching on junk food again, I couldn't bring myself to stop. After a while, I couldn't control the urge to have food in my mouth. Eventually, I gained back all the weight I lost, plus a few extra pounds.

I went through a deep depression when I found out my worst dream was becoming a reality. I didn't want to believe my weight was back where it started. I began to think terrible thoughts about myself, feelings that should not have entered my mind or anybody else's. I was feeling fat and ugly, and thought I had no reason to live if I looked this way.

At first I used to just lie in bed and cry myself to sleep. I'd have horrible dreams about death and how bleak the future would be if I decided to stay alive.

Things seemed so weird to me. I didn't want to do anything but stay in my room and cry. Sometimes I'd write poems about the way I was feeling, but that only made me more depressed.

"I was feeling fat and ugly, and thought I had no reason to live if I looked this way."

I realized I was getting worse. I knew I needed some kind of help. That's when I wrote a suicide note to my twin sister, Charlotte.

Charlotte didn't believe what I wrote. She said, "You're not going to kill yourself."

"Yes, I am," I responded.

"No, you're not, stupid!"

"Don't call me stupid!"

"You're just doing this for attention," Charlotte said as she walked out of our bedroom. I started to cry. The thought of my sister not wanting to comfort me made the whole situation worse.

The next day I gathered pills from all over the house and from our foster mother's bag. I didn't know what they were for, but I knew they would damage a person's body if they were taken all together.

When I had the pills, I put them all in a bottle and hid them underneath my pillow. Then I wrote good-bye letters to some of my close relatives.

The following day I gave Charlotte the letters. She went straight to our foster mother with them. Our foster mother came and asked me why I was thinking of doing something so insane.

I told her my reason. My foster mother said I was not fat, and that if I did succeed in killing myself, I would be taking a lot of people with me.

But I hadn't been thinking about the people in my life. I hadn't realized I wouldn't be hurting myself as much as I would hurt the people who loved me.

My foster mother was very angry with me for not telling her sooner what I was feeling. She held me in her arms and cried and told me never to think about killing myself again. She soon decided I should see a therapist. I didn't think it was necessary until I got there.

The therapist was nice. This wasn't my first time going to a therapist, but it was the first time I ever told anyone how I felt about my weight. I always knew I needed help, but I'd had no one to talk to about this issue.

I talked to the therapist for almost two hours. She helped me realize that life was more than looking a certain way. She said I was an intelligent, caring, and beautiful young adult, and that I should not let my weight be my burden. She also gave me a diet plan she had gotten from her doctor when she had to lose some weight. She said the diet worked for her.

> **"I realize I have a life to live, not just a body to get thin. I'm smart. I know that with my good brain I can be anything I want to be."**

The confidence and self-esteem I received in that one session gave me the hope of being the size 12 I wanted to be. (I haven't gotten there yet, but I'm working on it.) I only saw that therapist once, but she had a big impact on the way I look at myself.

I still worry about my weight a lot. Not one day goes by without me thinking about how I look. But now I don't take it to the extreme of thinking about suicide.

After sessions with several other therapists, I now know there's more to life than being slim like a model in a magazine. It would be nice to look that way, but it's also okay to have some meat on your bones. I realize I have a life to live, not just a body to get thin. I'm smart. I know that with my good brain I can be anything I want to be.

Many young women worry about the way they look. From their hair down to their toenails, they're always trying to make themselves look more appealing. It's okay to think about your body and how you present yourself, but only to an extent.

Young women should not make body image their first priority. Unless you want to become a model, you should be thinking about your education and your future career. Always trying to look good is not going to get you far in life.

So for you young women out there who think that being thin is all you need to get somewhere, try to apply this advice to yourselves: Having a slim body and pretty face are not enough to get you anywhere.

I may not be model material, but I am still a nice-looking person. I'm proud to be the way I am. And I'm not going to let anyone tell me otherwise.

CHARLENE JOHNSON was seventeen when she wrote this story. She is also the author of "A Mother to My Mother's Children" (page 136).

THINK ABOUT IT

- Think about something you struggle to accept about yourself. What helps you accept it?
- Think about a time you felt overwhelmed by a problem. What steps did you take to put the problem into perspective?

LOSING MY FRIENDS TO WEED

by Jamel A. Salter

I had a lot of friends I grew up with. Growing up together made us very close—until my friends got too close to weed.

Before that happened, we were always together. We'd go to movies, parties, the park. If we didn't have anywhere to go, we'd stay at one of our houses and play video games.

Even though we were close friends, we still had our little arguments. But when we argued, Dave would get in the middle and try to stop it. He was almost like the official peacemaker of the group. Dave also had the best sense of humor. He was always telling jokes. That was one of the best things about hanging with my friends—you always got a good laugh.

"I had a lot of friends I grew up with. Growing up together made us very close—until my friends got too close to weed."

But one day, when we were about fourteen, my friends made plans to put money in to buy some weed. I didn't want to put any money in, because I didn't want to have anything to do with weed. I thought, "If I don't put any money in, they'll say I can't smoke and I'll pretend to be disappointed." But they got enough money to go through with it and said I could smoke anyway.

Someone had to ride his bike thirty-five blocks to get the weed. (The things people do for drugs!!)

We were at the park when they started smoking. One person lit the blunt, took a puff, and passed it around. I was in total shock because I had read and seen about drugs on TV and here they were right in front of me.

As the blunt was going around I thought to myself, "What should I do? Should I say yes or no?" I looked at how my friends were reacting after they smoked. Since it was their first time, everyone coughed hard after they took a puff.

I sat at the end of the line, hoping they would finish the blunt before it got to me, or that someone else would turn it down so I wouldn't be the only one who refused. Neither happened, and I found myself being handed the blunt.

"Chill, yo, I don't want any."

"Take a puff, son, it's mad nice."

"If you don't smoke, you're a wimp."

"You can't be a mama's boy the rest of your life."

I got so tempted that I actually took the blunt in my hand. But I knew it was a choice between smoking and keeping their friendship or not smoking and keeping my health. I came to my senses and just passed the blunt on.

"You really are a wimp."

"You can't hang, mama's boy."

When they finished smoking, they started acting like fools. They were hitting each other and cracking stupid jokes. Seeing the way they acted made me glad I didn't smoke. The next day, everyone was talking about how bad they felt in the morning. You would think that would make them come to their senses and stop, but they just started making plans to get more.

My friends have been smoking for a year now, and it's changed them. They always look like zombies. Their eyes are always red and halfway closed. They have bad tempers, and they're always ready to fight. Especially Dave—now he has the worst temper of them all.

A few weeks ago we were at the park playing basketball. Dave had the ball. When I tried to steal it from him, I slapped his hand by accident. He got highly upset and started yelling at me.

"I knew it was a choice between smoking and keeping their friendship or not smoking and keeping my health. I came to my senses and just passed the blunt on."

"Why are you fouling me?"

"It was an accident. I don't know what you're getting mad about, anyway," I told him. "It's all part of the game. If you can't deal with it, don't play."

Dave tried to punch me, but missed. The others held him back and calmed him down. This surprised me because Dave was always the peacemaker before he began to smoke pot.

My friends and I used to play against other blocks in basketball, and I always started. I didn't hear about a game for a while, but I didn't worry. I figured my friends would tell me when they

"I wish our friendship could go back to the way it was before, but I don't think there's any chance of that happening while they keep smoking. I used to think they were true friends, but now I know it was just a game."

were playing. Then one day I was walking past the park and I saw them just finishing playing another team. I got upset—I always started and now, because I didn't smoke weed, they didn't even bother to call me. (By the way, they lost.)

Not being close to my friends like I used to be makes me think to myself, "Maybe I should smoke it just one time. What's the worst thing that could happen to me?" Then I remember the way they acted that day in the park and I just forget about it.

You might be wondering why I don't stop trying to stay close to them, why I don't make new friends. But it isn't so easy to lose friends you've grown up with. I keep trying to talk them out of smoking, because I don't want that stuff to make them sick. But they just laugh as if I'm stupid and tell me to mind my own business.

I wish our friendship could go back to the way it was before, but I don't think there's any chance of that happening while they keep smoking. I used to think they were true friends, but now I know it was just a game.

If my not smoking is the reason I've lost my friends, then I've been cheated. It's hard to believe that the difference between friends and no friends comes from one little blunt.

JAMEL A. SALTER was sixteen when he wrote this story.

THINK ABOUT IT

- Think of a time when you went along with the crowd, even though you didn't want to. How do you feel about the incident now?
- Think of a time when you stayed independent and didn't go along with the crowd. How do you feel about that incident now?

OUT, WITHOUT A DOUBT

by Xavier Reyes

Growing up, I always believed negative stereotypes about gays and lesbians. These stereotypes put down homosexuals and gave me an excuse not to educate myself about them. But when I got older, I learned that the only person I was dogging was myself. When I was twelve, I always acted macho and dogged girls and gays so my boys wouldn't think I was a "faggot." We never exchanged anything more than a handshake. I always thought if two guys exchanged something more than that, something was wrong.

> "When I was thirteen, my feelings about sex began to change."

I was extremely afraid of gay people. I believed all the lies I heard, such as that gays are not real men, they're sex maniacs, and they're all going to hell. Any time my friends and I saw a gay person, we'd make fun of him by walking "feminine."

But when I was thirteen, my feelings about sex began to change. For example, I once found myself looking at another guy and saying, "Damn, he's cute." When this happened, I tried telling myself it was wrong. I ignored my feelings, and they went away. At least I thought they did.

When I was fourteen, the feelings came back stronger. I thought it was just a phase, so I continued dating girls and putting down gays. At the same time, though, I was scoping out other men. I still believed there was no way I could be gay. After all, I didn't act like it.

It wasn't until I moved into my group home that I had my eyes opened. I was now fifteen and still afraid of gays. When I first moved in I knew there were gays there, but I never expected to have one as my roommate. Because I had allowed myself to fall for myths about gays, I was extremely insecure about having a gay roommate.

I wouldn't change my clothes in front of Mike. I began to sleep in more than just my boxers, and I never walked around in just a towel. I was scared that Mike might try to hit on me or give me a surprise wake-up call in the middle of the night and make me "less of a man."

This insecurity didn't last too long. I began to get to know Mike for *who* he was, not *what* he was. I found out that we liked the same music and loved going clubbing. I didn't feel like I had to prove something to get his respect. But when Mike asked me if I was straight or gay, I lied. I told him I was straight but had a couple of gay friends.

The reality was that I was faking it. I knew I had feelings for guys, but I just didn't want to come out with that. I was afraid of being put down. I didn't want people to think I was a sissy, but at the same time I felt miserable. I was sacrificing being happy for my reputation.

After getting to know Mike better, I felt a little more comfortable with my sexuality. I didn't have to put up a front when I was with him. I grew jealous of Mike because he didn't care what people thought of him. His motto was, "You get what you give." I wanted to be like him—out, without a doubt. I didn't want to live my life in a closet.

As much as I wanted to come out and be free, I still had a hard time accepting the fact that I was gay. I couldn't picture myself sleeping with another guy. I had always believed that straight men had to act masculine, play sports, and lie about the women they had sex with. They didn't have sex with each other. If a guy was gay, then he had to be extremely flashy and flamboyant, walk feminine, and listen to Madonna all day.

"I was sacrificing being happy for my reputation."

For some reason, Mike didn't seem to fit any of the stereotypes I had. He wasn't feminine, and he hated Madonna. Then it hit me. I realized I had prejudices about gays and lesbians and that, until I was able to free myself from them, I couldn't accept myself.

Mike really opened my eyes and mind. I saw that I didn't have to be feminine to come out of the closet. After about three weeks, I decided I was ready to unlock all the locks.

I called Mike into the bedroom and said there was something I had to tell him. I was a nervous wreck. I had sweaty palms, shaky knees, and a dry mouth. He saw how nervous I was and immediately closed the door and asked me what was the matter.

"Mike, I want to tell you something. Please do not tell anyone yet. Okay?"

"Okay," he replied with a concerned expression.

"I, I, I'm, well, there's a chance that . . ."

"What is it?" he asked, getting more and more anxious.

"Well, I could be, you know . . ."

"Know what?" he asked.

"I might be . . ."

He looked at me with this "I know you're gay" look and asked me to finish.

"I'm, well, um, I'm gay."

I swear, the minute I said that, I felt so relieved. I finally felt I had no more hidden secrets. It's strange, but it felt like I could even breathe a little bit easier now that I'd gotten this off my chest.

First, Mike laughed. Then he looked at me.

"Oh, I knew that," Mike said with his usual "I know everything" tone of voice. "I was just waiting to see when you were going to come out."

"I felt so relieved. I finally felt I had no more hidden secrets. It's strange, but it felt like I could even breathe a little bit easier now that I'd gotten this off my chest."

I looked at him and said, "Then how come you never told me?"

His reply was, "I don't know."

Mike was the first person I told I was gay. He promised not to tell anybody else. I didn't tell anybody else either for a couple of days. I was still trying to accept who I was. Just thinking about having a boyfriend or lover made me shake my head in disbelief. I was going against everything I thought I believed in.

About a week later, I came out to the other gay residents. I always received replies like, "It's about time," and "You need to get a man." Because my gay friends were supporting me, I decided to take my chances and tell a straight female friend.

"You're what?" Mary asked in disbelief.

"I'm gay," I repeated.

"Boy, you need to stop playing."

"I ain't playing. I'm dead up," I replied.

She looked at me and said, "You ain't one of 'em 'cause you don't act like it."

"Act like what?" I asked. By this time she was really making me mad.

"You know," she said, putting her hand on her hip. "Fem."

"Just because I'm gay doesn't mean I've got to act fem," I said.

"Well, in my book you do, 'cause guys like you aren't gay."

I looked at her and walked away.

When I thought about it later that night, I kept asking myself, "Why should I have to be fem just because I'm gay?" I finally made up my mind that I was going to be me, regardless of what anybody said. No one could tell me how to act.

I began hanging out with my gay friends more often. We went to clubs, the Village, and lots of gay house parties. I met kids my age who were out of the closet. Some were extremely feminine, while others were straight-up roughnecks. Either way, I grew really confident about myself.

> "I finally made up my mind that I was going to be me, regardless of what anybody said. No one could tell me how to act."

When I came out to the staff in the group home, they couldn't believe it. One staff member even said, "A good-looking guy like yourself is gay? Boy, I hope there are some men left out there for my daughter." It seemed like the more I told people, the more I wanted to come out.

Eventually, I made sure the whole world knew. I didn't want to live my life in a closet. I had pride in who I was. The only person who didn't know was my mother.

My mother and I have always had a bad relationship. I ran away from home when I was thirteen. When I was growing up, she always spoke against gays. She used to say they needed mental help, it was immoral to be gay, and it was just a phase. Believe me, I was not running to tell her anytime soon that I was gay.

When I was seventeen, I ran away from the group home and moved in with an older friend of mine. My friend was also gay. The agency called my mother to let her know I had left care to live on my own. They gave her my telephone number and one morning she called me.

"Hello," I said, trying to shake the effects of deep sleep from my head.

"Xavier, this is your mother!" she screamed at me. "Do you know what you're doing?" she asked, her voice higher than it was before.

"Listen, Ma, this is my life. I'm tired of being in a group home!" I screamed back at her, shocked that I actually yelled back for once.

"Well, who are you living with?" she asked. I could tell she was taken aback by my tone of independence.

"A friend, Ma," I replied, trying to figure out where she was going with her questions.

"I don't know about you. But I find it pretty strange that you're living with another man!" she screamed at me.

"Ma! What do you want?" I replied.

"Is he doing anything to you?" she asked.

By this time I was really upset with her.

"No, he's not doing anything to me," I said.

"Then why are you living with him? Are you a homosexual?"

I paused for a minute, debating whether or not I should tell her. I was mad scared, but I felt this would prove to her that I was my own person. I knew there was only so much thinking I could do, so I let my mouth make the decision. "Yes, I am a *homosexual*," I said, emphasizing the word.

"Although my mother didn't accept the fact that I was gay, I still felt relieved I'd told her. I had no more secrets from her. She knew who I really was."

Then my mother tried to tell me I needed help. I, of course, pointed out that homosexuality is not a mental disorder. Then she tried telling me how society wouldn't accept me. I told her I didn't care what society accepted. After that, she tried dissing me by telling me I wasn't a real man. I told her straight up:

"Ma, the last time I checked below my belly button, everything was still intact. Who I decide to sleep with is my business, not yours. As long as I'm not sleeping with anybody you know, that part of my life has nothing to do with you."

She hung up on me.

Although my mother didn't accept the fact that I was gay, I still felt relieved I'd told her. I had no more secrets from her. She knew who I really was. I wasn't bothered by her negative attitude toward gays. We didn't have a relationship before I came out, so it really didn't matter if we still didn't have one after I came out.

It took three months for my mother to speak to me again. Although we still don't have a close relationship, she has come to accept me. She's told me she's extremely old-fashioned but that she knows times have changed. She's also told me that since there's nothing she can do to change my sexuality, she has no choice but to accept it.

"Of all the things I have learned, the most important is that I cannot allow stereotypes or prejudices to come between me and the rest of the world."

We had that talk eight months ago. Now she has taken the easy way out: Don't ask, don't tell. Whenever I do talk to her nowadays, she doesn't ask, say, or even suggest anything about me being gay. It bothers me, but I also understand that in her own way she has accepted me for who I am.

Of all the things I have learned, the most important is that I cannot allow stereotypes or prejudices to come between me and the rest of the world. I've learned the hard way that I should never judge a book by its cover. Ever since I've come out, I try to get to know people for who they are, not what they are.

I'm not scared anymore to tell people I'm gay. In fact, I enjoy telling them. I don't fit the stereotypes people have about gays, and that really makes them stop and think twice. I never know when I might bump into someone who could be going through what I went through. The least I can do for them is be out of the closet.

XAVIER REYES was seventeen when he wrote this story. He graduated with honors from his high school, worked for the Stonewall Foundation, and received a college scholarship. He left foster care to live independently after seven years in the system. Xavier is also the author of "My Struggle with Weed" (page 93).

For more about where Xavier is now, see page 169.

THINK ABOUT IT

- Have you ever hidden your true identity or feelings because of what others might think? What did that feel like? Did you eventually reveal who you really are? If so, what happened?
- Are there things about yourself that you wish you could tell a sympathetic friend? What are they?

I'M BLACK, HE'S PUERTO RICAN . . . SO WHAT?

by Artiqua S. Steed

It's funny how I met my boyfriend. I was walking down the street with my best friend and my sister when this guy rode by us on a bike. I noticed him right away. He had a caramel-colored complexion and very pretty eyes. He looked kind of like my father.

I tapped my friend and told her I thought he was cute. So she turned around and called him. "Hey! Hey, you! On the bike!" He turned around. "Yeah, you, come here. My friend wants to talk to you." I was very embarrassed. I couldn't believe she'd actually done that.

But it worked. The guy started to come back toward us. I'd thought he was a light-skinned black, but I saw as he came closer that he was Latino. I thought to myself, "It must be really dark out here for me not to have noticed before that he's Puerto Rican." But since he was cute I didn't really care.

I was very nervous. I didn't even ask him his name. All I could say to him was hi, so he took over the conversation. He asked me my name and how old I was. We talked for a few minutes, and then he asked me for my number. I didn't want to give it to a guy I didn't know, but I took his.

> **"I'd thought he was a light-skinned black, but I saw as he came closer that he was Latino."**

When he gave me the paper I looked down at it and it said Johnny. "Johnny," I thought. "What kind of name is that?" It was so plain. I'm used to very unusual and unique names. Besides, I thought he would have a Hispanic name.

He told me to call him the next day at three. As I walked away from him, I had a huge grin on my face. When I finally caught up to my sister and my friend, they started laughing at me. But I didn't mind.

I called Johnny the next day around three, like he said. The phone rang and then a recording came on. I was mad. How could he tell me to call and then not be there? I called him back about twenty minutes later. This time he answered.

We talked for two hours about everything. He told me about himself and the things he liked to do. He told me that he was a DJ and also wrote songs. He also told me about his background—his father is half Chinese and half Puerto Rican.

"I didn't know what I was getting myself into—him being Puerto Rican and me being black. I'd never had a serious interracial relationship before, and it caught me by surprise!"

After three days of conversing on the phone, we finally decided to see each other again. When he came to meet me, he was on his bike. (I learned later that he's attached to that bike—he won't go anywhere without it.)

We had a nice time, even though we only went to his house. He made me a playlist of all my favorite songs. We spoke to each other every day after that. After three or four weeks, he asked me to go out with him. I said yes before he could finish his sentence.

I didn't know what I was getting myself into—him being Puerto Rican and me being black. I'd never had a serious interracial relationship before, and it caught me by surprise!

I'd thought about the issue of dating someone of another race, but could never imagine myself doing it. I was always very into black pride. I thought any black man who considered another woman more beautiful than a black woman was crazy. And I strongly believed that a black woman who dated a man of another race was ignoring how hard black men had to work to get where they were. For black women to give up on black men would be totally wrong, I thought.

But when I met Johnny my attitude started to change. I still have pride in my race, but I came to realize that if a black woman dates a man of another race, it doesn't mean that she's given up on black men. And thinking that black women are more beautiful than women of any other race is just going overboard.

I have to admit that the fact that Johnny isn't black is one of the reasons I started liking him so much. I thought it would be a new experience to date someone who wasn't black. I was excited to learn more about him and his background, culture, and beliefs. I wanted to see the world from his perspective. I even found myself trying to learn Spanish.

At first, it was hard to look at him and not see his color. But as I got to know him, I found Johnny to be no different than any black male I have known, except that he's Puerto Rican and speaks Spanish.

Not everyone saw it that way. In fact, my brother and sister and some of my friends gave me a hard time for going out with Johnny. Whenever I called him, my brother would say things like, "Why are you on the phone with that guy?"

> **"I have to admit that when Johnny and I first started going out, it was hard for me to get past my own stereotypes about Puerto Ricans."**

My sister was even worse. She's what you would call a bigot. She feels there's no need for anyone in her family to be dating someone who isn't black.

My best friend once asked my sister, "What would you do if I married a white man?" My sister's exact words were, "Don't bring him to my house." She told me she didn't like Johnny, and I knew it was because he's not black.

I have to admit that when Johnny and I first started going out, it was hard for me to get past my own stereotypes about Puerto Ricans. I thought they had no color coordination (my sister always said they were the ones who came outside with mismatched colors and no socks), that all they liked to eat was rice and beans, and that they were always copying black fashions and music.

Before meeting Johnny, I often found myself having conversations that were critical of Latinos. I remember one time when my sister and I saw a Puerto Rican couple fighting on the street. The guy was hitting the girl. I said to my sister that if the girl had been black, she would have fought back. My sister agreed with me.

I thought that Puerto Rican girls were brought up to think it was okay to take beatings from their husbands and boyfriends. I never considered that the girl was just scared of her boyfriend, and that's why she let him hit her.

Now when I hear racial slurs against Puerto Ricans, I'm offended by them. I've learned they're not true. It hurts me when people dis Puerto Ricans, because they're talking about my boyfriend.

Whenever my friends and family do it, it makes me feel bad. They don't see that they're talking about someone I care a lot about. The other day, I snapped at my sister for saying something stupid about Puerto Ricans. I don't remember what she said, but I know it made me mad.

Johnny's family has never said anything against me or our relationship, as far as I know. Some of his friends even told him they thought I was pretty and asked him if I had any friends for them. He does have one friend who doesn't like *morenas* (a Spanish name for dark-skinned girls), but I've never met the guy and he hasn't done anything to come between us.

"Now when I hear racial slurs against Puerto Ricans, I'm offended by them. I've learned they're not true. It hurts me when people dis Puerto Ricans, because they're talking about my boyfriend."

I have learned to get past the stupid comments of family and friends, but outsiders still get to me. People are so ignorant. For instance, when Johnny and I went for a walk downtown recently, people would not stop giving us dirty looks. Just about anywhere we walk, people stare. I don't know if Johnny notices it, but I do! It gets annoying after a while.

We also hear people say how interracial relationships are wrong and leave "culturally illegitimate" children (meaning, children who don't belong to any race). Those are the kinds of things that get to me.

Johnny and I have been going out for several months now and we get along fine, considering the racial difference. I feel he respects me more than any other guy I've dated. This doesn't have anything to do with the fact that he's not black; it's just the type of person he is.

Most of the guys I dated in the past were only interested in me for one thing. They didn't care about making a commitment or being sensitive to my feelings. But Johnny has shown commitment. I've never caught him cheating on me, and he never likes for me to be upset at anything or anyone.

Of course, our relationship isn't perfect. There are a lot of things we can't agree on, and we argue about them. For one thing, I can't see why he won't get a job. He wants to stay in the music business and thinks that working on getting a record deal is enough for now.

But the fact that we are racially different doesn't bother us. Like they say, love is blind; it doesn't see color. If you ask me, being of different races hasn't made our lives together more difficult, but more interesting. For example, it's fun for me to try to figure out what in the world his mother is saying when she talks to Johnny in Spanish. (I even speak a little Spanish myself now.)

> "If you ask me, being of different races hasn't made our lives together more difficult, but more interesting."

The hard part is dealing with other people's attitudes. Interracial dating is still hard for a lot of folks to accept. But if two people are in love or like each other a lot, then racial or ethnic differences will not wreck the relationship.

Since I'm happy, I can put up with being called a *morena* by Johnny's friends. I can stand having people tell me I'm in love with the wrong person.

ARTIQUA S. STEED was sixteen when she wrote this story. For more about where Artiqua is now, see page 169.

THINK ABOUT IT

- Have you ever been accused of going against your racial, ethnic, or social group? If so, what was the experience like?
- Think of a person or situation that caused you to change a strong belief. Did the experience lead you to question other beliefs you had? If so, how?

RELATIONSHIPS

CONNECTING WITH PEOPLE WHO MATTER

RELATIONSHIPS are connections with other people based on sharing, mutual respect, and openness.

The opposite of building **RELATIONSHIPS** is cutting yourself off from others, protecting yourself by hiding behind a false front, or valuing other people only for what they can do for you.

RELATIONSHIPS are hard because you must *give* of yourself as well as *take*. **RELATIONSHIPS** require you to take risks and trust others.

RELATIONSHIPS give you understanding, friendship, and sometimes even love.

Relationships, our third resilience, are close and fulfilling ties to people who matter. Relationships don't just happen. They deepen slowly over time. To form a relationship, you have to balance giving and taking, helping and being helped. You have to have as much regard for someone else's well-being as for your own. You risk the possibility of being rejected. You let another person see your weaknesses and know your private feelings.

Relationships are a resilience because they help you connect with others who value you. Relationships provide a sense of belonging, opportunities to express yourself, and support when you need it. In a strong relationship, your friend's face is a mirror where you can see yourself as lovable, capable, and worthy, rather than alone and unnoticed.

The stories in this section are by teens who are working hard to relate to people who matter—other teens, family members, other adults. You'll see them taking risks to form lasting relationships. They've learned that when you have deep connections with people who know and value you, it's easier to meet challenges and solve problems.

NOT A GIRL AT ALL

by Anonymous

I am bisexual and transgender, and I have conservative, religious immigrant parents. At school, most of the teachers and students call me by my chosen name and pronouns, which are *he/him*. But everyone in my family and at my temple thinks I'm a straight girl and knows me by the name my parents gave me when I was born. It sounds like a stranger's name in my mouth; it doesn't belong to me.

I first realized that I am bi and trans in middle school. I had been aware for a long time that I liked both girls and boys, but since I had no name for what that was, I ignored those feelings. This changed when I went online and began to follow people who posted about the LGBTQ community. Then I discovered a YouTube channel by a transgender guy. In his videos, he talked about gender dysphoria, which is a term for the distress a person can feel when their physical body doesn't match the gender they identify with. When he described dysphoria, it resonated with me. That's when I realized I wasn't a girl at all.

> "Knowing I was part of the LGBTQ community made me feel happy and proud . . . But I knew my parents wouldn't understand."

Knowing I was part of the LGBTQ community made me feel happy and proud, like I belonged somewhere. But I knew my parents wouldn't understand, so I had to keep it from them. My relationship with my parents was already distant; they weren't big on showing emotions, and I feared I would disappoint them if they found out.

In seventh grade, I mustered up the courage to tell my friends that I didn't think I was straight, or a girl. To my surprise, neither mattered to them. Coming out to my friends was like telling them what I had for lunch that day. I could tell that they thought of me as the same person—just one with a new name and pronouns, who liked both girls and boys.

Fortunately my friends and teachers were supportive. My guidance counselor didn't tell my family I was trans. She encouraged me to join our school's gay-straight alliance (GSA). By talking to people in GSA, I learned that not every LGBTQ kid has a family that accepts them. It was a relief to know I wasn't alone.

Though I was starting to express my true identity at school, I still felt a lot of self-hate. I knew my family viewed people like me as freaks of nature. When I told one of my teachers that, he said: "Are you going to live for them or for yourself?"

I told him that I felt like I was committing a terrible act of betrayal against my parents just by being who I am. My teacher replied that I was walking around as if I had a mask on, and that hiding my true identity was making it impossible for me to see the good parts of the world. He said it wasn't my fault that I felt this way, because someone had put this metaphorical mask on my face at a young age and superglued it there. He said I was not worth any less than anyone else because of the people I love or the gender I identify as. I had never heard that before. I didn't believe him at the time, but I fell in love with his words and his promise that one day the mask would be lifted.

"I felt like I was committing a terrible act of betrayal against my parents just by being who I am."

One day in eighth grade, my dad shoved open my bedroom door and slammed it behind him. My room is tiny, so there was practically no space separating us. I felt like a wild animal trapped by a game hunter.

"Give me your phone," he said. He sat on my bed, scrolling through my chats and browser history.

I walked out and waited on the living room couch, my palms sweaty and my heart pounding. I felt a sick feeling rising in my throat.

Finally he called me back to my room and made my mom stop cooking and sit with us. He sat me on his lap—"just like when you were a little girl," he said—and smoothed my hair out of my eyes. Tears rolled down my face. I could see that he knew.

"She's talking to people online," he said to my mom. "She's watching all these gay things and now she thinks she's one of them."

"I'm not gay, Dad, I'm bisexual, and it means I like girls and boys," I pleaded, staining my father's polo shirt with my tears. I thought maybe if I weren't "fully" gay, he wouldn't think it was that bad. Maybe he could accept that I wasn't going to change.

My mother interjected, "What do you know? Have you even kissed anyone? You go to temple every week, and you were practicing sin all along."

"She thinks she's a boy too," my dad went on, his eyes wild and cruel. "Would you like me to show you how to tie a tie? Do you want me to call you my 'son'?"

My mom batted at my dad's arm, telling him to stop. I thought she would defend me, but she just said, "Stop mocking her. Her mind is damaged."

Then my dad's eyes softened and he said I could repent for my sins. I'm ashamed to say that all I did was cry and nod my assent. Yes, I would go to temple more frequently. I would wear dresses and be the girl I never was.

"I worked hard to maintain my image as a straight girl at home."

For months afterward, my parents watched me closely to make sure I acted "like a girl." I actually enjoyed expressing my more feminine side, but no matter how much lipstick I put on, I didn't feel like a girl.

To stop my family from finding out that I was still using a different name and pronouns at school, I worked hard to maintain my image as a straight girl at home. I asked my mom to teach me how to cook so that I could make food for my future husband. I went to services on Sundays and tried various eye makeup looks. Slowly my parents started to believe I was turning into the perfect young woman.

My sixteenth birthday came along, and all my internalized pain came exploding out of me like a piñata. I got my makeup done, bought a tiara, and put on a fluffy pink dress. I batted my lashes and collected my birthday money, but on the inside, I wanted to scream.

Last year I started seeing a therapist after a school counselor called my mom to recommend it. My mom drives me to therapy every Sunday because she sees that I'm stressed, but she doesn't understand why I prefer talking to "outside people" rather than my own mother.

The fact that my therapist is bound to confidentiality makes it easier for me to open up to him. Even though he isn't trans, he has helped me acknowledge that trying to ignore and repress my gender dysphoria only makes things worse.

> "Healing is a process, and I look forward to moving on in my life. But that doesn't mean I'm betraying my family by being myself."

I still experience a lot of pain due to my situation. I'm still frustrated that I can't express myself the way I want to while I'm living at home. It feels so unfair. But what has changed is my ability to deal with this frustration.

Now when I am overwhelmed by negativity, I recognize what I'm feeling and accept those emotions rather than judging myself. I distract myself by watching a movie or writing a poem. Healing is a process, and I look forward to moving on in my life. But that doesn't mean I'm betraying my family by being myself.

I don't know exactly how I identify on the spectrum of gender and sexual orientation. And I still don't know if I'm going to keep up contact with my family after I graduate and leave their house. But as my therapist says, I don't need to have all the answers right away.

ANONYMOUS was sixteen when he wrote this story.

THINK ABOUT IT

- Have you ever had to choose between being true to yourself or putting up a front to please your parents? Which did you do and why? Did you try to explain yourself to your parents? Why or why not?
- Have you ever considered breaking off your relationship with your parents? Why? Would you have done it if you had someplace else to go? Does it take more courage to break away or to stay and tolerate your difficult home life? What would it take on your part to keep up a relationship with parents who don't accept you as you truly are?

SHE'S MY SISTER (NOT FOSTER)

by Tamara Ballard

Most of my life I've wished for a sister. I'd always heard that having a sister wasn't a bowl of cherries, but I like to learn things the hard way.

I've been in foster homes with other girls, both older and younger, but I didn't have much of a sisterly relationship with any of them. That changed when I moved into my present house.

My new foster mother spoke highly of Cheryl, a foster child who had once lived with her. She said she wanted Cheryl back, so I wasn't really surprised when I came home one Sunday and saw Cheryl's suitcase in the hallway.

> "Most of my life I've wished for a sister."

For a while after Cheryl came back, I continued to share a room with another foster girl, Ericka. Cheryl shared a room with our foster mother's two biological kids. But things really were not going well with Ericka, so I wasn't surprised when she got kicked out.

Soon enough, Cheryl was my new roommate. I was really cool about her moving in, just as long as she stayed out of my way. Don't take this wrong, but I was used to having my own room. In my previous foster home, I had my own room for four years. I never felt threatened by Cheryl—it just felt weird to share a room. After all, I had just gotten out of a bad roommate experience with Ericka.

The only thing I really envied Cheryl for was the respect our foster mother's biological kids gave her. They didn't have that respect for me. (They still have no respect for me, but it's better than it used to be.) I guess they have so much respect for her because they've known her longer.

Since Cheryl had a job and went to school, we never really talked. We either didn't speak or, if we did, we argued. We had a lot of disputes because we were two totally different people who never took the time to get to know each other. We basically lived on a "hi and bye" basis.

Sometimes we'd have an actual conversation. We'd talk about basic stuff, like what was for dinner or the weather, nothing personal. Despite our conversations, I still looked at her as just a roommate.

Before I got to know Cheryl better, I thought she was too bossy. The thing that bugged me the most was that she was always telling me to clean the room. I'm a clean person, but she's cleaner. Another thing that caused arguments is that there's no telling Cheryl no.

One night during the summer we had an argument because I did something she didn't like. Cheryl, my cousin, and I were watching TV when Cheryl asked me to get a glass of water for her. I didn't feel like going, so she asked my cousin. My cousin also said no, so Cheryl demanded that I go. So, with an attitude, I went. The only reason I did was because it was late at night and I didn't want to hear her mouth.

I came back with a half-gallon bottle of water, but it was almost empty. I put the bottle down and with a real snotty attitude I said, "Here's your water. It should last you a while."

> **"Before I got to know Cheryl better, I thought she was too bossy."**

My cousin started laughing, but Cheryl gave me the glass she was using and demanded that I wash it out. In my now nasty mood, I took the glass, put some water in it, and threw the water out the bedroom window so I didn't have to go out of the room again. Then I poured some more water in the glass and handed it to Cheryl.

She said she didn't want it, so I started to finish off the water by drinking it from the bottle. This made Cheryl furious! She said it was a nasty thing to do and smacked me on the hand as if she were my mother and I was a little kid! Needless to say, that started another argument.

When I complained about her, my foster mother told me that was simply the way Cheryl was, but I didn't want to hear that. I have one mother—my biological mother. If I didn't listen to her, I wasn't gonna listen to someone who didn't have anything to do with me. Cheryl was just a roommate. She wasn't anything to me, and she didn't have any papers that said she was my guardian.

I don't know at what point things changed, but somehow they did. They changed for the better.

Somewhere along the line we started to talk. I noticed we liked the same things. Despite what went down, she was my roommate, and I realized that if I put down my guard, we might actually have a friendship. For example, Cheryl and I like to watch the same TV shows. We also have one thing in common that will never change—we are in the foster care system together.

I began to see that we were sailing along in the same boat, only she was more equipped than I was and I needed her. She had been in the foster care system longer. She knew the way things worked. All the stuff I was doing, she'd already done.

So I tried a new approach with her. I started to look at Cheryl differently. She's a good influence on me. After all, she's three years older, and she's in school working on her GED (General Equivalency Diploma). She's very smart and has her life in perspective.

"I began to see that we were sailing along in the same boat, only she was more equipped than I was and I needed her."

She knows what she wants and goes for it. That's like her motto. With anything (clothes, music, guys), if she wants it and it's available, it's as good as hers. I don't know how she does it—I think it's part of her personality.

I don't look at Cheryl as just a roommate anymore. Now I look at her as a sister and a friend. We've started talking about boys, school, food, personal stuff. We talk about everything biological sisters talk about. Occasionally I go to the store where she works and help her. We are equal—there is no better or worse when it comes to me and her.

We share secrets and ask each other for advice—about boys, mostly. I tell her stuff that even my social worker doesn't know. Cheryl knows when I cut a class or have an argument with a classmate, a teacher, or one of the girls. I also complain to her about my boyfriend, William. She does the same with me. Our sisterly relationship is a two-way street.

The other night I wanted to know what Cheryl thought of me.

"Cheryl, what do you look at me as?" I asked her.

"A sister," she responded.

"Not foster?" I responded in amazement.

"Nope."

I was happy that the feeling was mutual.

Cheryl, as my sister, has taught me that behind the labels "foster" and "roommate" there is an actual person. And with this actual person, a relationship can grow that lies deeper than the foster care system.

TAMARA BALLARD was sixteen when she wrote this story. She later lived in Augusta, Georgia, where she was an honors student in high school and played volleyball. Tamara is also the author of "Walking Out the Anger" (page 120).

THINK ABOUT IT

- Have you ever known someone who you started out disliking, but who then became a good friend? What led you to change your mind about this person? How did you develop a friendship?
- Think of a time when someone labeled you and then assumed to know something about you. How did it feel to be labeled?

BONDING THROUGH COOKING

by Aurora Breville

When I entered foster care at age thirteen, I didn't know how to cook. There were a couple of simple things I could probably have prepared if I was given the ingredients. Other than that, I truly didn't know my way around the kitchen.

My first foster home was pretty cool because it was just girls living there. That meant not waking up to a raised toilet seat and no funky feet! It also meant being able to talk without worrying about being misunderstood. I couldn't picture talking to a couple of guys about how my heart got broken on a date, while making a casserole with an apron on.

Imagine the chaos in a kitchen with a bunch of boys and girls together. SCARY! So, at the same time I got my first taste of cooking, I was able to share my thoughts and feelings for the first time and bond with girls my age.

I remember the day they found out I couldn't cook. I walked into the kitchen and saw one of the girls making something that wasn't familiar to me: Ramen noodles. I stared into the pan, trying hard to see past the foam, and asked in disgust, "What is that?"

"Imagine the chaos in a kitchen with a bunch of boys and girls together."

The girl gave me a look that said, "Are you for real?" Then she told me what it was.

I asked her, "How do you make that?"

At first she couldn't believe I'd asked her how to make Ramen noodles. But after about five minutes of stirring the flavor packet into the pan, she told me gruffly, "Get yourself a pan and fill it with water."

Then she said, "Wait for the water to boil and add the noodles. Let it boil for three more minutes and take it off the stove. Are you gonna eat it with the broth?"

I said, "No."

"Then you're gonna need the colander."

"The what?" I asked, perplexed.

"The colander, the strainer, the metal thing with the thousand holes and a handle. You have to use that to drain your noodles." And with that she stalked out of the kitchen with her lunch.

The other girls came strolling into the kitchen soon after she left. One by one they started throwing questions at me.

"Do you know how to make fried chicken?"

"Do you know how to make eggs?"

"Do you know how to clean meat?"

"Do you know how long to fry bacon?"

As they fired these and other questions at me, I shook my head no. The questions went on and on, and my answer never changed. I honestly expected them to make fun of me and say all sorts of things behind my back, because I was the new girl who didn't know one thing about cooking.

That was not the case, however, and I'm very glad I was honest with them. I could've lied about being able to cook, but then I might've made a major mistake like burning the house down. That wouldn't have been cool.

My next cooking lesson came after the girls heard our foster mother complaining that I was walking around the house grumbling about a growling stomach. I had the nerve to take it a step further and ask my foster mother, "When are you going to cook dinner?"

My foster mother took one look at me and said, "I don't cook for grown women. I'll cook once in a while when I feel like it, but otherwise you go in there and fix yourself something to eat. And close the door on your way out."

"I could've lied about being able to cook, but then I might've made a major mistake like burning the house down. That wouldn't have been cool."

I went into the kitchen feeling dejected and hungrier than ever. I looked through all the cabinets and in the refrigerator. Everything I saw had to be prepared and cooked in some way, shape, or form. I was ready to give up and go to bed hungry for the first night in my life when "The Cooking Squad" came on the scene.

"Whatcha doin', Li'l Bit?" Diane asked.

"Just lookin' for somethin' to eat," I said, "that's all."

"You can't be looking for something to eat, child. You don't have pots and pans out, number one. And number two, you didn't put anything on the counters ready for cooking."

"So what do you want to eat, girl?" Lena asked.

"I don't know yet," I replied. "I'm still trying to decide."

"Why don't you make some macaroni and cheese to go with that chicken left over from yesterday?" Diane suggested.

"Yeah! And you can add some mixed vegetables on the side, you know, to get the vegetable portion out of the way," Kayla offered.

My mind was reeling at this point. I was hungry, and I was going to cook for myself?? For real??? Get out of here!

I wanted to continue my strict ritual of waiting patiently for someone else to cook for me, something I'd done for thirteen years running. Why break such a delightful cycle? I thought there was nothing wrong with being pampered for one more year. The idea of cooking for myself was revolting. I tried my hardest to get the girls to follow through with the food suggestions they made.

"My mind was reeling at this point. I was hungry, and I was going to cook for myself?? For real??? Get out of here!"

Bad move!

They made me feel like I should've been arrested for asking someone else to cook for me at my age, and concluded by saying something that made me (and my stomach) mad: "I guess you're not all that hungry then."

"Fine!" I snapped. "Then show me how to cook the stupid thing, doggonit!"

Laughing, they told me to get out all the ingredients I needed to make my first dinner: a bowl of leftover chicken, a cup of milk, a pat of butter, the box of macaroni and cheese, and the frozen pack of mixed vegetables.

I don't have to tell you how bad my stomach was growling. I felt like it was trying to scrape my back! It was hard to concentrate, but I tried following their instructions as much as I could.

I cooked the macaroni first and left it on the stove so it could stay toasty warm. I warmed up the chicken in the microwave for three minutes. I did the mixed vegetables last, since they take the least amount of time to cook.

My very next cooking lesson involved something I swore I would never do in my life: cleaning meat. These three girls were determined to change my mind about that—and fast!

I was eating a bowl of cereal one morning when Diane, the oldest, came into the kitchen. I made a move to leave when she yelled, "Freeze!"

Of course you know I sat right down and waited for her to bark.

"I gotta teach you how to clean chicken."

Not a "Good morning, did you sleep okay?" Not even a "What's up?" She was determined to get right down to business and didn't care what I thought.

As if on cue, Lena and Kayla came into the kitchen, pretending to be sleepy-eyed.

"What are you gonna do with the chicken, Diane?" Kayla asked.

"Nothing. She's gonna clean the chicken for dinner tonight."

Kayla looked at me, looked at Lena, and just went to the refrigerator for the milk to go with her cereal.

Lena was nice about the whole thing. She came over to where I was sitting and asked, "Have you ever cleaned chicken before?"

I shook my head no because my mouth was full of cereal.

"It's not hard," she continued. "All you need is a knife and some hot water. Show her, Diane."

"Come over here."

I walked over to the scene of the crime. When I got to the kitchen sink, Diane handed me the knife.

"Pick up the wing and take off the skin with the knife."

I looked at her, looked at the wing, and started to pull the skin away.

When I was finished, I put the wing in the waiting bowl and stared at Diane.

"Do the rest of them," she commanded and walked over to the refrigerator.

As I was finishing the rest of the chicken parts, she handed me the lemon.

"Use the lemon to season the meat after you wash it off in hot water. DO NOT use the dishwashing liquid—the hot water's enough."

Believe me, I was not dumb enough to use the dishwashing liquid to wash meat. I knew I didn't want to taste any soap on my chicken. Personally, I think she was just saying that to be mean.

I thought everything I did was wrong, but when everyone sat down to fried chicken that evening, they licked their fingers and asked for more.

I thought I was in the clear after that night. Wrong!

My next lesson was to make breakfast for the whole house on cleaning day (Saturday).

Diane came into my room at eight in the morning.

"Wake up, sleepyhead," she said, shaking me. "Come with me to the kitchen. I got something else to teach you."

I gotta tell you that at this point the barking stopped. Diane started talking to me just like any other person. I guess she started having respect for me since I put a hurtin' on that chicken the last time I cooked.

The lessons weren't all bad either. While I'd cleaned the meat, Diane had asked me questions, like where I lived, what kind of music I liked, and if I went to church. I found out that Diane hadn't lived too far from me before she came into foster care. We also liked the same kind of music: everything except country and heavy metal.

"I thought everything I did was wrong, but when everyone sat down to fried chicken that evening, they licked their fingers and asked for more."

This time when Diane took me to the kitchen, Lena and Kayla didn't follow, which was another shock. I guess they figured they wouldn't get any more laughs out of me since I knew (somewhat) what I was doing.

Diane got all the things I needed to start my first big breakfast: eggs, bacon, sausage, bread, butter, milk, orange juice, and the box of pancake mix.

"Get the big frying pan out of the bottom cabinet."

While I got that, she told me about the latest episode between her and her "boo," Derrick.

"You're gonna make pancakes with bacon and sausage. Put the bread in the toaster last. And do you know what he said after I threw his shirt at him?"

"No. What?"

"He said, 'You think I wanna keep this shirt after you stank it up?' Now I had to start swinging 'cause you know I don't stink, as good as I'm smelling when I walk out of here!"

I couldn't help but laugh at that one. She thought I was laughing because she had to teach her man some manners, but I was really laughing because he had a point about that shirt!

"I felt wonderful whenever it was time to cook because it also meant doing something that my parents had never encouraged in my thirteen years of living with them: bonding with other girls my age."

While Diane talked and laughed about all the things her boyfriend said and did, I prepared the batter and the pan for my pancakes. After the entire batter was finished, I fried up all the bacon and toasted the bread last, just like she asked.

When I was finished, I felt proud of what I made with my hands. My taste buds and stomach were pretty happy with what I did too. It made my heart feel good to see Kayla, the heartiest eater of the house, ask me, "Can you show me how you made your pancakes so golden brown? Mine always come out looking funny and sick!"

When I was alone that evening, I couldn't help but puff up with pride. It actually felt good knowing there were dishes out there that were no longer a total mystery to me. I felt a little more like an adult because I didn't have to depend on anyone. I always thought that cooking for myself would be such a chore because of my huge appetite, but it really wasn't!

I felt wonderful whenever it was time to cook because it also meant doing something that my parents had never encouraged in my thirteen years of living with them: bonding with other girls my age. It was another adventure for me that held many ups and downs, both in and out of the kitchen.

Today I really can't tolerate having people in the kitchen when I'm making something, but I don't forbid it. Whenever I'm cooking, I feel like I'm working on something that will help to make a bigger and better me.

I've definitely come a long way from macaroni and cheese, and I'm no longer cheesy inside about cleaning meat. And making friends has become second nature to me because, just like cooking, it's no longer a crazy idea.

AURORA BREVILLE was nineteen, living in a group home, and planning to go to college when she wrote this story.

THINK ABOUT IT

- Think of a time when you made a friend through doing something together. Do you think you would have become friends with this person if you hadn't gotten to know each other through the activity?
- Think of a time when someone taught you a skill you didn't know. What was it like to admit you didn't know something, be willing to learn, and trust the other person to teach you?

A LOVE TOO STRONG

by Tamecka Crawford

I had to fall flat on my face before I learned I was alone in this world. I came from a home where there was no love shown. At night I'd sit up in bed and cry. There was no one to give me a shoulder to lean on when I needed support, a pat on my back when I did something good, or even a sympathetic ear when I failed.

My father passed away when I was eight, and one day my stepmother simply never returned home. I went to live with my paternal grandmother and then a maternal aunt, but neither living situation worked out. I felt like someone had cursed me, like there was a dark cloud hanging over my head.

When I was sixteen, I came to a group home. For the first time I met people who really cared about me, who accepted me without judgment, who gave me the love and attention I needed.

But the first few months at the group home were hard. I was very scared. I didn't know how to act, whether or not to close myself off from people. Back home I was so used to nobody caring that I just stayed alone in my room. I wasn't used to receiving love and attention, but the staff made it hard for me to stay isolated.

"When I was sixteen, I came to a group home. For the first time I met people who really cared about me, who accepted me without judgment, who gave me the love and attention I needed."

The staff got involved in my everyday life. They were always interested in hearing about what was happening in school or my social life—things my family never asked about. We had Independent Living class once a week, and the teacher always made it very interesting. She would ask us questions to get us to open up about our feelings.

One staff member in particular, Ms. Thomas, really touched my heart.

The first week I got to the group home, Ms. Thomas called a house meeting for all the girls. We discussed many things, such as boyfriends, the staff's behavior toward the girls, and age differences among the residents.

I can remember all twelve of us sitting around the living room. Ms. Thomas wanted us to talk one at a time, but every time someone spoke there were at least nine interruptions from people who disagreed. Ms. Thomas became very upset with our disrespectful behavior. Everybody was pointing at each other and getting overexcited, the phone kept ringing, and it was just crazy.

Suddenly Ms. Thomas began to cry. It was the first time I had ever seen anyone cry for someone else. It showed me how deeply she cared for us, how much it bothered her that we didn't care for anyone but ourselves.

Since I never had anyone take such an interest in me before, I began to admire Ms. Thomas dearly. The rest of the staff did nothing except what they were paid to do. But Ms. Thomas was always there to listen, to see how she could help us. She encouraged us to visit our families and checked up on how we were doing in school. I found myself getting very attached to her, but one day she was transferred from my house to another house within the agency.

> "Since I never had anyone take such an interest in me before, I began to admire Ms. Thomas dearly."

When Ms. Thomas left, I closed myself up again. I began to stay to myself and hide in my room. I felt she was the only person who could ever take away my feelings of being unloved. She seemed the only one who accepted me as I was, who knew my needs, and now she was gone.

The funny thing is, Ms. Thomas didn't know how I felt about her. When the staff told her how I had closed up again, she acted very cold-hearted whenever she saw me. As I later realized, Ms. Thomas felt I had become too dependent on her, that she could never be the "perfect mother figure" I'd imagined. I didn't want her to be distant from me—I wanted her to love me back. I hated her for letting me down and hated myself even more, because I had no control over my feelings.

I was scared, and I went through an emotional hell. I had flashbacks to the time I lived with my family, the time when nobody cared. My family had felt that if I had a roof over my head and clothes on my back, there was no need to say, "I love you." I dreaded the return of that lonely feeling.

Ms. Smith, the director of social work, went to war with me over my attachment to Ms. Thomas. She kept reminding me that my feelings were very unrealistic and that it was inappropriate for me to act and feel that way toward an agency staff member.

I despised Ms. Smith for telling me that. Although at times I knew deep in my heart that she was right and really cared about my well-being, I stood firm. I couldn't face being unloved again, and I was terrified at losing Ms. Thomas. I was more determined than ever to win back her attention.

"I've learned to open up to those who are willing to open up to me, but at the same time not to mistake their kindness for a parent's love. That's a kind of love that can never be replaced."

I still admire Ms. Thomas. My feelings for her go up and down like a roller coaster. I realize that Ms. Smith was partly right, that my expectations were unrealistic and sometimes unfair. But on the other hand, my attachment to Ms. Thomas was just another bond that had been broken by the foster care system. I was searching for love and attention, no matter how they came.

As a victim of the system, I have learned never to take anything for granted and that relationships aren't always permanent. I have learned not to count on too many people, but to look within myself for guidance and security. That way, if anyone disses me, I won't be disappointed.

I've learned to open up to those who are willing to open up to me, but at the same time not to mistake their kindness for a parent's love. That's a kind of love that can never be replaced.

TAMECKA CRAWFORD was nineteen when she wrote this story. She later went to college, an experience she describes in "College Can Be Hell," (page 96).

For more about where Tamecka is now, see page 169.

THINK ABOUT IT

- Have you ever wanted to be close to someone who didn't return your strong feelings? How did the situation turn out? How do you feel about that experience now?
- Have you ever known someone who expected more from you than you could give? How did you feel about this person's expectations?

LEARNING TO FORGIVE

by Christopher A. Bogle

Every time I saw my mother, we would argue. She'd bring up things that happened in the past and throw them in my face. I found it hard to forgive her for the problems that led me to end up in a juvenile detention center. My social worker, Ms. Davis, knew my relationship with my mother was not good and urged me to go to therapy. Ms. Davis wanted to see us get along better.

I didn't want to go to any "stupid" therapy. I felt I'd be wasting my time, because my relationship with my mother wasn't going to get better.

Ms. Davis told me I had to go to therapy because it was part of the services I was supposed to receive while I was in the foster care system. I felt I was being forced to do something I didn't want to do. But I finally decided to go, because I didn't want to be sent to another group home.

I started seeing Ms. Smith on Saturdays. I could see she had a nice personality from the way she spoke to the kids and their mothers. The first time, we spoke briefly in her office. She was very patient, and I felt comfortable talking to her. She explained that she wasn't going to try to rush me into expressing myself about my problems with my mother. She wanted me to get to know her better before I started confiding in her.

> "I didn't like talking about my problems. I felt I couldn't trust anybody."

I didn't like talking about my problems. I felt I couldn't trust anybody. I had been hurt a lot by many loved ones who were supposed to be in my corner when times got rough. They let me down big-time by misusing my trust.

By going to therapy each week, I started to express myself better. I took my time telling Ms. Smith about my problems to see if I could trust her. I told her it was going to be difficult forgiving my mother because I was still carrying so much anger.

Whenever my mother tried to call me at the group home, I would tell the staff I didn't want to speak to her. She'd leave messages for me to call her, but I didn't want to have anything to do with her. I had been making it without her, so why did I need her now? When I saw her on the streets, I would walk past her without saying anything.

The reason things got this bad between us was that my mother treated me the same way my father treated her. My father verbally abused my mother. He would belittle her every time they argued. I always felt my mother took out her anger toward my father on me. I found it harder to get along with her than my sisters did. She always treated me differently from them. She went shopping with them and spent time with them, but not with me. I reacted by spending a lot of time away from home.

One Saturday, Ms. Smith wanted me to talk about why I ended up in a detention center. I told her that one night my mother and I got in a huge fight when I came home very late and talked back to her. My mother got real upset and tried to hit me with a chair. When I blocked it with my hands, the chair fell back on top of her. She then tried to hit me on the head with a glass vase. My sister's boyfriend got in front of me and blocked her swing with his hands. The vase cut his hands so badly that he had to go to the hospital for one hundred stitches.

"The first step in forgiving someone is to really mean it from the heart."

I got upset while I was telling this to my therapist. She stopped me for a minute so I could calm down. I was very emotional and frustrated.

When we continued, I told Ms. Smith how my mother came to court and accused me of cutting my sister's boyfriend with a piece of glass. She also told the court that I hit her with a chair and that she had to go to the doctor. I was locked up in a detention center for two weeks before going to a juvenile prison for a year and a half. I felt a year and a half was taken away from me for no reason.

Ms. Smith told me that I had to learn to forgive my mother and release the pain inside me. She said the first step in forgiving someone is to really mean it from the heart. I heard what she said, but I didn't know if I was ready to make that first step. I didn't know if I was ready to open up my heart to my mother and forgive her.

I left therapy that day feeling like a better person. I'd finally gotten the chance to release some anger by talking about my problems. During my ride on the train, I thought about my mother and what Ms. Smith said about forgiving. I knew everybody makes mistakes and deserves a second chance.

My mother called me around seven o'clock that same night. Lisa, one of the staff workers, asked me if I wanted to speak to her. I took the phone and told my mother that we needed to talk things out. My mother agreed, and she sounded very good. She wanted me to come to the house after school.

I went to see my mother the next day. I wanted to talk to her about our problems. I'd realized as I got older that I was at fault for some of them. I never listened to anybody, and I wanted things to be done my way. I knew I had to stop feeling sorry for myself for ending up in a detention center. I wanted to tell my mother how sorry I was that I didn't listen to her and that I was disrespectful to her. I wanted to tell her how I felt about her as a mother, how I wanted to start a new relationship as mother and son.

She was cooking dinner for my two sisters when I walked in the kitchen. My mother asked me how I was doing in school and in my group home. I was nervous to be under the same roof with her, because this was the first time in two years that I was able to come home to visit. I didn't want the same thing to happen as happened last time, when the cops had to remove me from my house. I went into my big sister's room to talk with her until my mother was finished cooking.

"I thought about my mother and what Ms. Smith said about forgiving. I knew everybody makes mistakes and deserves a second chance."

My mother called me from my sister's room to have dinner and talk with her alone at the table. She told me how sorry she was for coming to court and seeing me end up in a detention center. She said she'd been hurt by the way I treated her that night. I told my mother that I forgave her and that I wanted to start a new relationship with her and just move on.

I could see tears running down her cheeks when she told me I was the only son God gave her and she loved me tremendously.

I stood up to hug my mother because I knew she really meant every word she said.

My relationship with my mother is much better now. We're able to communicate better, and we get along well. I can go to the house any time I want and eat. I can go home on weekend passes, and I spend all the major holidays with her.

The reason our relationship has changed is that we both realize everybody makes mistakes and deserves a second chance. I had to accept that I couldn't just blame my mother for what she did. If I had listened to her when she told me to come home early, she would never have gotten so worried and angry.

I'm glad my relationship with my mother has improved, but we still have problems. I'm able to deal with them better and talk about them without holding any negative feelings inside. If it weren't for therapy, our relationship wouldn't have changed. I just wanted her to love me the same way she loved my sisters.

My mother and I started going to therapy together to try to prevent what happened in the past from ever happening again. It was hard being in therapy with her because I was afraid she would get mad if I said something she didn't like. My mother is the type of person who gets offended easily and is not afraid to defend herself. When I was in therapy alone, it was easier to express myself and the room was less tense, but eventually I got used to being in therapy with her. We spoke about the problems we had in the past. I felt wonderful because we were able to communicate and be in the same room together.

"The reason our relationship has changed is that we both realize everybody makes mistakes and deserves a second chance."

I feel our relationship is better, but I wouldn't want to destroy it by rushing home before I'm ready. I want to take it slow. But if something terrible happened to her health and she needed me at home to take care of her, I wouldn't even think twice about packing my bags and going to be by her side. I love her with all my heart.

CHRISTOPHER A. BOGLE was eighteen when he wrote this story. Later, he attended Long Island University for two years and then went on to graduate from Marine Corps basic training. Christopher is also the author of "Controlling My Temper" (page 21).

For more about where Christopher is now, see page 169.

THINK ABOUT IT

- Have you ever forgiven someone who'd hurt you badly? If so, how did you feel? If you haven't been able to forgive the person, how does that feel?
- Think of someone with whom you have a difficult relationship. What makes the relationship difficult? What steps are you willing to take to improve it?

INITIATIVE

TAKING CHARGE

INITIATIVE is taking action, meeting challenges, solving problems.

The opposite of taking **INITIATIVE** is giving up or feeling helpless.

Taking **INITIATIVE** is hard because some problems seem too overwhelming to solve.

INITIATIVE helps you see that you can make a difference in your own life.

Initiative, our fourth resilience, means facing life's challenges head-on. When you take initiative, you begin a positive cycle of solving problems, overcoming fears, and being a winner. Knowing you've met challenges in the past boosts your confidence in the future. When problems come your way again, as they certainly will, you'll know you can handle them. Initiative is a resilience because it puts you in charge.

Like many people, you may find initiative much easier to talk about than to practice. Sometimes inner voices tear you down. They tell you you're not capable, that it's too risky to try. It seems easier to avoid problems by seeing yourself as a victim. Being a victim may get you sympathy and keep people from criticizing you.

Taking initiative is always a risk—you could fail or look foolish. All the writers in this section choose to accept that risk. They've learned to take initiative and solve problems. Initiative helps them see their problems as challenges they can overcome.

IT TAKES WORK TO FLIRT

by Danny Gong

Flirting. It's one of the necessities of a teenager's life. It's such a powerful skill and the first step to attracting that special someone.

But how does it work? How can you harness its power? Most important, how in the world do you start?!

Flirting is like a game. The only way it works is if you practice. Trust me on this, I know. Before I bought a book called *101 Ways to Flirt*, I had some big problems with flirting. I didn't know the first thing to do. (Okay, so I still don't.)

All I know is that it's gotten easier over time and with practice.

Don't ask me why I bought the book. It was kind of spur-of-the-moment, and of course I wanted a girlfriend. But I'm glad I bought it, because that book has actually helped boost my confidence. It's taught me how to be approachable and how to tell who's flirting with *me*.

There's nothing wrong with getting a little help, even if people insist that flirting should come naturally—because sometimes it doesn't. That doesn't mean you'll always be a bad flirt. It just means you may have to work at it—like me.

> **"Flirting is like a game. The only way it works is if you practice."**

During the early stages of my adolescence, I was a quiet, shy, hang-around-the-same-group type of kid. Everyone in my group had the same haircut and the same clothing style, with expensive name brands plastered across our bodies.

We even had the same taste in girls—ones who pretended to have high-pitched, little-girl voices and who tried to be innocent and cute while milking us for money.

Our flirting technique made me nauseous. The same procedure, the same style. No adrenaline. No direct contact (at least not in the beginning). When you liked a particular girl, the only flirting was an ultra-quick, lightning-speed, blink-of-an-eye stare, and that was it. Then came the detective work.

After you'd initiated the nanosecond look, you'd find out as many things as possible about the person from friends who knew other friends who knew her friends. You'd get all the information you could—from brand of underwear, to school, to the people she knew. Not until you did private-eye work and dug the whole dirt could you even approach the girl.

But I got sick of playing it safe. I wanted to open myself up to a larger world. I wanted to be open and loud. So first I changed my appearance.

I cut my hair short and styled it really funky, gelled and sticking straight up. I gave my wardrobe a spice of different clothing, like postal workers' pants. People even said my voice sounded different.

Then I changed my flirting style.

The first time I seriously got into the game was when I was fifteen. I tried—well, sort of. It was a failure. I was in-line skating in a park after school. I'm a pretty good skater, so I tried showing off a bit. I caught the eyes of a few girls. Then I found one I thought was particularly interesting and started to advance very slowly toward where she was sitting.

"But I got sick of playing it safe. I wanted to open myself up to a larger world. I wanted to be open and loud. So first I changed my appearance."

I was really nervous, and I had to pee. What a bad combination. I talked to myself constantly.

"Should I?"

"Why not, Danny? You can do it."

"Nah, I'm just going to look like a fool."

"Come on, you big chicken. Do you want to be a single pathetic fool in his late forties, looking at porn magazines and downloading sex pics off the internet? Are you that sad? Huh? Are you?"

"All right! Shut up. I'll do it."

So for the next half-hour I skated back and forth trying to be obvious, building up my guts, getting ready to say something. Finally, some words came out of my mouth.

"Huh . . . Hey . . . Hi, there . . . Um . . . (cough, sniff, scratch at nose). Ahem . . . Urgg . . . So, hey. What's your name?"

There was no answer.

"See, she didn't answer! I look like a fool now."

"You idiot, do you expect her to hear you from fifteen feet away?!"

I moved closer to her. This time I was shaking, biting my lips, scratching my head.

"Ahem, huh, hi."

She was talking to a friend so she didn't pay much attention, and I also spoke so low that I might as well have been talking to myself.

"Hi." It was just a little louder.

She turned and looked up.

"Excuse me?" she said.

"Do you have the time?" I know, I know. It's such a cheesy line, but I had to say something.

"What?"

"Do you have the time?" Drops of sweat were running down my forehead. I should have put on some extra deodorant.

"Yeah, it's 4:45."

"Thanks."

And that was it. I went skating off, my heart still racing, my head throbbing. They got up and left.

So my first attempt was pretty sad, but I had to start somewhere. Besides, little failures like these can help you find out what to work on, how to avoid the same mistakes, how not to be so devastated when you do get rejected.

> **"Little failures can help you find out what to work on, how to avoid the same mistakes, how not to be so devastated when you do get rejected."**

After that incident, I didn't do much besides look. I didn't want to feel like a moron again. But after being pestered by my conscience, I worked myself up and decided to try again.

I had some small successes, like one time when a girl on the subway talked to me for a while. But in the end she didn't give out her telephone number. I felt like there was a big "Rejection" stamped across my forehead.

But I coped with it and continued to flirt—which was the most important thing. I figured it was like fishing. You just had to be patient. You cast your style of bait. Within two seconds you could get a bite, or you could stand there all day with a few nibbles here and there. You can only do so much to attract the fish, and when you finally do catch one, you just might throw it back into the pond. But you have to continue to try.

Then one day I was in a store with my friend Peter, and I saw *101 Ways to Flirt*. I figured, "Hey, why not?" Peter made fun of me. When I asked him if he wanted to chip in, he said, "No!" I was talking a little loud so he was probably embarrassed.

"When it gets right down to it, flirting can be pretty complicated."

"Why not? It looks fun, and you could use a couple of tips yourself considering you go to an all-boys school," I said.

So he agreed.

It seemed like it worked as soon as I bought it. The cashier took one look at the book and smiled at me. I shrugged and smiled back.

"It's not for me," I said defensively.

"Yeah, right. Are you sure you need this?" she asked, waving it around.

Hey, if that ain't flirting, I don't know what is. If just buying this book got a conversation going, think of what could happen if I read it.

The book doesn't guarantee you can find that special someone, but it gives you enough tips so you can increase your chances. The authors offer concrete tips like, "Good flirts don't ever make contact with body parts other than eyes."

The only thing I disagreed with is that the authors make flirting sound easy. When it gets right down to it, flirting can be pretty complicated. For instance, even though smiling is sometimes a form of flirting, it isn't always. If someone's just very smiley, you can get the wrong idea—which can make you a little depressed when you find out the truth.

Still, the flirting book has helped me get over my anxiety and control my fears. Before I got the book, I'd ask myself a lot of questions, doubt myself, and go through other nonsense that got in the way of a potential good flirt. Now I more easily come up with a question to start a conversation. I've even come up with lines besides "Do you have the time?"

I hear a lot of people say, "Why do you need a book? What, are you desperate?" But the fact is that for some people who aren't born with high charisma, books can help. What's wrong with a little assistance?

So if you buy a flirting book, don't think of it as, "I'm desperate, I can't get a date." Think of it as, "Hey, I'm smart, gonna get me some more dates and meet new people."

Flirting books are like the *Princeton Review* of dating. They don't guarantee a perfect 1600, but they can raise your score.

DANNY GONG was seventeen when he wrote this story. He went on to attend college, write plays, and become an actor.

For more about where Danny is now, see page 169.

THINK ABOUT IT

- Think of a problem in your life that you once viewed as hopeless, but eventually solved. What helped you solve it? What changed your view of the problem?
- Have you ever taken initiative by reading a self-help book for advice on solving a problem? If so, what was the result? If not, would you consider using a self-help book someday?

MY STRUGGLE WITH WEED

by Xavier Reyes

When I was thirteen, I had a lot of problems with my mother. She abused me, and I stole things from her to get revenge. It got so bad I ran away from home and lived on the streets for three months.

During those three months I started smoking weed. I did it to get my mind off my troubles. And since I had a lot of troubles, I smoked a lot of weed.

Sometimes I smoked weed with my crew, other times I smoked it by myself. I usually got high after the first blunt, but if I didn't, then two more afterward did the trick.

Every time I got high, I would go through the same stages of reliving memories. Some of these memories were very violent, while others were calm and quiet.

For example, I always got very quiet after I smoked my first blunt. I'd sit down and think about the times my adoptive mother abused me and called me "negro" and "black boy" just because I had black friends. As I remembered her verbal abuse, my anger would begin to build. I'd get mad and become very violent because the weed made these memories so vivid. When I was high, it seemed as if the abuse happened yesterday. I got so angry that I'd call people names and try to fight them if they answered back.

"Every time I got high, I would go through the same stages of reliving memories. Some of these memories were very violent, while others were calm and quiet."

"Hey, you got the time?" I once asked this guy when I was high.

"No," the guy said. He just kept walking.

"You know why you ain't got the time? 'Cause you too damn poor to buy a watch!"

The guy stopped and looked at me like I was crazy.

"What did you say?" he asked, as he came toward me.

"Chill!!" all my homies said. They jumped in front of him and told him I was crazy. I was in the back, yelling at them to let him fight me, but my homies made the guy walk away.

After I'd try to fight someone, I'd run around, knock over garbage cans, and chase cats into the street so they'd get hit by cars. This stage lasted about two hours.

Then, just as the high was ending, I would enter a stage where I felt depressed and guilty. I'd blame myself for getting abused. I'd cry until all my tears were gone. Then I would wipe my eyes, get high again, and go through the same moods all over again.

Fun, wasn't it?

By getting high, I was only trying to block out all the pain I felt from living on the streets. But the only thing that smoking weed did was bring back bad memories. Instead of blocking out the pain, it only made it worse.

Yet I kept on with my weed smoking. I didn't want the bad memories to disrupt my pleasant high. But no matter what I did, I couldn't stop them—memories of a childhood that was always sad and filled with gloom. A childhood filled with abuse, neglect, and racism from my adoptive mother. Nights when I went to bed without food or water, days when my adoptive mother made me wear the same clothes over and over without changing them. Memories that haunted me every time I'd get high.

"By getting high, I was only trying to block out all the pain I felt from living on the streets. But the only thing that smoking weed did was bring back bad memories. Instead of blocking out the pain, it only made it worse."

I felt so tortured that I decided there was only one way out—to quit smoking. The high was excellent, but if giving it up meant that the horrible memories wouldn't haunt me, then I figured I could live without it.

It took a lot of patience to quit. I was really addicted. It was like a champion boxer giving up the sport at the peak of his career.

Day after day I'd try to think of something to do to help me quit. The craving was unbearable. It was like finding a million dollars on the street and then having to give it back.

Sometimes when I felt like getting high, I'd go to sleep or eat a lot. Other times I'd take long walks. Then I got a new girl, so I was able to take my mind off weed.

I stopped hanging out with the people who smoked weed. If they offered me any, I told them no. There were times when I wanted to smoke so badly I would've offered any amount of money to someone to get it for me. But I knew I had to stop if I wanted the memories to stop.

After about seven weeks of suffering, the craving finally disappeared. It seemed like it happened overnight. One day I was dying to smoke, the next morning I couldn't even stand thinking about it. I finally realized that weed hadn't done anything for me but put me through seven weeks of pure hell.

That was two years ago, and I haven't picked up a blunt since. So you see, there's another reason why people stop smoking weed, other than getting busted or because of what it physically does to their bodies. Nobody ever talks about the inner feelings they have when they smoke weed. No one ever talks about the bad memories or feeling paranoid or guilty. If they did, people would understand that smoking weed doesn't make pain go away. It only makes it come back twice as hard.

My story may seem odd, because not many people come forward and tell the real reasons why they quit. Well, I may start a trend!!

XAVIER REYES was seventeen when he wrote this story. Not long after the events he writes about here, he went into the group home he describes in "Out, Without a Doubt," (page 48). Xavier says, "When I had my problems with weed, I wasn't yet out as a gay person. My two stories show how much I've grown and changed over the years."

For more about where Xavier is now, see page 169.

THINK ABOUT IT

- Think about a habit you have. What purpose does it serve? Does it help or hurt you? Do you want to get rid of it? Why or why not?
- Have you or someone you know ever taken steps to stop some harmful behavior? What qualities do you need to take control of your life this way?

COLLEGE CAN BE HELL

by Tamecka Crawford

Going off to college for the first time can be a scary experience for anyone, but especially for a foster child. We don't have the support of a parent, and a lot of times we feel as if we're alone in the world. Before I left for community college, I wondered what college life would be like for me.

Although I wanted so badly to be independent, I still wanted someone there to fall back on. How would I survive all alone in a strange place? Also, could I make it as a "college student"? Would I fail or drop out? I worried about people finding out I was from a group home and treating me differently or making fun of me. I even wondered if my professors would treat me differently.

Although I had gone on several college tours and seen the campus of my school before I went there, I was still nervous. I was anxious to know if I would be compatible with my roommate or if we would have problems.

When I first started, things seemed fine. I had six classes, and the workload was all right. But then I met a guy and started spending lots of time with him, skipping classes and not studying. I felt I had all the time in the world to pull my grades up. So I slowed down, missing classes I didn't like. I started having trouble, and my grades dropped tremendously in history and math.

> "Although I wanted so badly to be independent, I still wanted someone there to fall back on. How would I survive all alone in a strange place?"

I found myself using the excuse of being in foster care every time I missed a class or failed an exam. I would say to myself, "Oh, I'm from a group home. Who cares if I go to class or not? Who cares if I fail an exam or even if I pass one?"

I felt as if the words *group home child* were hanging over my head. Even though nobody treated me differently, in the back of my mind I felt they did. Like at the bursar's window (the place that deals with your bills), I felt they were hesitant to deal with me because they knew I was in foster care.

My self-esteem was very low. I sometimes just gave up and didn't care. As a result, I completed my first semester with a 1.0 grade point average (a D average) and ended up on academic probation my second semester.

I felt nobody cared for me. And it showed. I felt this way because I didn't have any family support. I kept making the mistake of comparing my life to the lives of students who had parents calling often and coming to visit. These students got care packages filled with all sorts of things, including their favorite foods, money, and supplies they asked for.

I wanted so badly to have someone care about me like that. I felt neglected, not to mention jealous.

I remember hearing my roommate talk on the phone with her mother, describing her day and what classes she liked. I wished so badly that I were my roommate, talking to my mother or to somebody who really cared for me. Although I did stay in contact with people from my former group home and with my junior high school dean, they weren't a substitute for family.

"Just before the end of the first semester I realized I had wasted time feeling sorry for myself and had to do something about it."

Just before the end of the first semester I realized I had wasted time feeling sorry for myself and had to do something about it. I never thought the semester would go so quickly. Like I said before, when you first get to college you think you have all this time. Then before you know it, it's over.

Gradually I realized that time was passing me by. I was so wrapped up in worrying about having people do things for me and care for me that I wasn't taking the time to care for myself.

I got tired of using the fact that I was in foster care as an excuse. I was tired of failing my exams. I was tired of crying. At the same time, I noticed that the people I envied weren't doing so well in their classes either.

I finally realized it wasn't because I was in foster care that I was failing my classes. It was because I had been paying too much attention to what people thought of me and how they treated me, and too little attention to my schoolwork. I had to accept the fact that I was in foster care. I had to move on. It wasn't being from a group home that was holding me back—it was me holding myself back.

The group home would soon be part of my past. I didn't want to fail in college because people didn't show me any "support." (Which sounds funny, now that I look back and think of the problems people face in this world, like children being abused and neglected.)

It was right after spring break that I decided to wipe my eyes and find ways to start my independent life. The first thing I decided to do was attend all my classes Monday morning and start pulling my grades up.

In my second semester my grade point average shot up to 3.25. I was studying night and day, especially subjects like history, which I always had problems with. I worked with a tutor, and I also found peer tutors (fellow college students who were good in a particular subject) to help me. In exchange, I'd type a paper for them or make them dinner.

"It was right after spring break that I decided to wipe my eyes and find ways to start my independent life."

I started letting professors know I was having problems. Some of them would meet with me privately to help me. Or if they saw I was struggling, they would let me know by saying, "I see your grades are dropping again. Are you having trouble studying?" Some gave me methods or extra materials to use.

My next step was to get counseling. When you're on academic probation, you automatically get group counseling. I'd had counseling in the group home, but I never liked it because I felt we were prejudged. But in college I felt it would help to have a one-on-one counselor. I realized I needed help dealing with the transition from the group home to college life.

I had a nice counselor who listened to me talk about school, my group home, and other things on my mind. At the end of the sessions, she would give me suggestions on how to deal with my problems. She helped me realize that while I couldn't have the family relationships I wanted so badly, I could thank God for the people who were taking the time to help me any way they could.

I also got a part-time job to make some extra money when the group home couldn't help me pay for whatever I needed. I was even able to put some money in the bank for rainy days. Basically, I started trying not to depend on the foster care system too much.

By my third semester in school, I was no longer seeking as much support from the agency or my social worker (everyone in foster care has a social worker). I was trying to make it on my own. I continued to go to counseling because I found it a very big help. Through counseling, I realized that just because people live with their biological families does not automatically make their lifestyles better than mine. I also realized that in some ways, being a foster child was an advantage for me.

For example, living in a group home was a big help in adjusting to college life because I had already learned how to live with a variety of personalities and attitudes. Also, I had already learned a sense of independence. Just like in a group home, when you're in college you have to do things for yourself and make sure things are getting done.

"Through counseling, I realized that just because people live with their biological families does not automatically make their lifestyles better than mine."

One thing that was easier for me when I was living in the group home was that everyone has something in common: Your family can't or won't take care of you. You all understand that and can talk about it. But in college you meet people from all sorts of different backgrounds, and sometimes you feel envious of their lifestyles. When other students were planning their spring breaks in Hawaii or Virginia, I was deciding what movie I was going to see during the break or whether to go visit a relative or stay in the group home. Sometimes I would just end up at the group home the entire time.

I learned that in order for anything to change, I first must care about myself. Then I'm able to care about the situation and do what I need to do. I'm looking forward to finishing my last semester.

TAMECKA CRAWFORD wrote this story when she was twenty-one, after she left the group home she describes in "A Love Too Strong," (page 77).

For more about where Tamecka is now, see page 169.

THINK ABOUT IT

- Think of a time when you felt sorry for yourself because of hurtful things that happened in your past. How did feeling that way affect you? What steps did you take (or could you take) to get over those feelings?
- Have you ever felt jealous of people you thought had it easier than you did? What steps did you take (or could you take) to stop comparing yourself negatively to others?

POETRY BROUGHT OUT THE PERFORMER IN ME

by Shaniqua Sockwell

When I was younger, I had no real creative outlets. I couldn't dance to save my life. I could sing okay, but not well enough. Any sports that required physical contact were out of the question.

But I always loved reading and writing. When I was little and got lonely, books were always there when I needed them. They were always willing to share their knowledge. The first book I read was *Little Women*. And if I wanted to share what I felt inside, I would pick up my pen and write down my feelings.

"When I was ten, I discovered my love of writing and poetry. I began to write because I wanted to express my feelings."

When I was ten, I discovered my love of writing and poetry. I began to write because I wanted to express my feelings. I learned how to write poetry by studying the poetry of Robert Frost, Maya Angelou, Langston Hughes, and Ntozake Shange.

From there I developed my own style. I liked to use metaphors, and I didn't like to sugarcoat the subjects I wrote about. My poems came from my imagination and from things I saw. I'd sit and try to come up with little verses. Most of the time they rhymed.

My first poem went like this:

The World Is a Gem

On the smallest island, in an oyster shell
    there is a pearl, that grows and grows.
It dwells beneath the emerald sea
    as green as grass can ever be.
Up above the flowers grow
    as fiery red as rubies glow.
And up above in sapphire skies
    diamond stars are drifting by.

I wrote that one when I was eleven. I liked comparing things with nature. I also wrote another poem called "Brown-Eyed Susan," in which I compared a flower to a girl.

As I matured, I began to write about deeper issues, like love, child abuse, rape, incest, the destruction of nature, black men and women being neglected in this country, politics, sex, war, and myself. Some of the poems were about personal experiences, but most were not. My inspiration came from things I saw in movies or real life, or books I read.

Sometimes when I finished a poem, I'd be shocked at how strongly I felt about the issues I addressed. But nothing scared me more than when I decided to read my poems out loud before an audience.

"Sometimes when I finished a poem, I'd be shocked at how strongly I felt about the issues I addressed."

When I was a junior in high school, I discovered a small café called the Living Room, which held poetry readings once or twice a month. It was right near my school, so I'd pass it on the bus. I was always interested in poetry readings, but I'd often heard the audiences were tough. I didn't think I was ready for that. I thought maybe this crowd would be easier to handle.

So I went in to the Living Room one day after school and asked about the readings. I was kinda nervous, but what did I have to lose by asking? They told me to call ahead of time to reserve a place on the list.

When the day came, I called and reserved my spot. I can still remember my number: twelve. Being the shy person I am, I couldn't believe I was doing this. But there was no turning back now. I wound up going alone because nobody was free to go with me. The reading was at eight.

I arrived and sat down. The room was small and narrow, but the place was packed. For some strange reason, I hadn't become nervous—yet. But I was feeling a little jittery. Maybe it was because I was the only black person in the room. Or maybe it was because everyone in the room was slightly older than me. But I wasn't going to let the way everyone was staring and whispering get to me. I was there to enjoy myself, read my poetry, and have a good time.

> "I wasn't going to let the way everyone was staring and whispering get to me. I was there to enjoy myself, read my poetry, and have a good time."

As I looked around, I was sort of surprised at how the place looked. The café felt like someone's living room, with antique chairs and tables, and bookcases with lots of books and magazines. They served every kind of gourmet coffee you could think of, and even the way they served it was cool. Instead of drinking from cups, you drank from bowls. But I just had a hot chocolate.

I had planned to read three poems, but after seeing how many people had shown up, I thought maybe I should just read two: a love poem and a poem about being lonely.

As the night progressed, I found myself feeling more relaxed and comfortable. The poems people read were really good. Some were funny, like the one a man read about looking into the toilet bowl. And some were sad, like the one a woman read about losing her sister to a disease. Some made you feel sorry for the person, like the one about staying with a man who's cheating on you. Some were just too long, like the poem a gay man read about being with his lover, which was four or five pages long!

But all in all I was enjoying myself, and nothing was going wrong. I was anticipating my turn. The crowd was nothing like I'd thought it would be. They were pretty supportive. I didn't have a care in the world until . . .

I heard them call my name. Now it was time to get nervous! My palms were sweaty, and I actually started shaking! But I couldn't back out now. So I walked away from the corner I'd been hiding in all night and got ready for my big moment.

I walked up to the front of the room and went to the mic. The guy had to adjust it for me since I'm short, and when I pulled the mic from the stand, I hit myself in the mouth with it. I tried to cover up my clumsiness by cracking a joke. I said, "Don't you wish these things came in sizes?" It was corny, but the crowd burst out laughing, which relaxed me.

"A lot of people don't share their talents. They keep them bottled up because they feel they aren't any good. I know how they feel because that's how I felt about my writing and my poetry. But I finally decided it was time I came out of my shell and showed everyone what I was made of."

I smiled back at everyone and said, "Hi, my name's Shaniqua, and I'd like to read everyone a couple of poems. Is that cool with you?"

The crowd said yeah, so I began to read. One poem I read was called, "In My Heart You Shall Forever Remain," about two lovers having to leave each other. The next was called "A Cry in the Night," about a young girl being physically abused.

As I read, I felt my nervousness gradually fading. I continued to read with no worries whatsoever.

When I finished, the crowd applauded. I was so happy I'd done such a good job. People came up to compliment me. I felt so good I decided to continue doing the readings.

Eventually, I moved on to other places. I now perform at the Moon Café on Friday nights. The environment there is really nice. The people are open and friendly. A lot of their poems are read out in rap style, or they're very cosmic. A lot of them deal with having to go back to the African motherland. There are a lot of black people there, but sometimes there's a mixed audience. There are paintings and sketches on the walls that you can buy, and instead of clapping when a performer's done, you snap your fingers. I like it a lot, and now that I've performed before, I no longer get nervous in front of big crowds. I'm far more relaxed and I take it all in stride.

A lot of people don't share their talents. They keep them bottled up because they feel they aren't any good. I know how they feel because that's how I felt about my writing and my poetry. But I finally decided it was time I came out of my shell and showed everyone what I was made of. Performing in front of an audience is as important to me as writing poetry. There's nothing like hearing people applaud and seeing them give you a standing ovation after you've read something you've created. It's a real thrill, and I get a lot of satisfaction from it.

Writing will always be my first love, and I will continue to write so I can get even better. I dream of winning a Pulitzer Prize or becoming a best-selling author. I'd love to be able to say that I've become everything I aspired to be. I haven't gotten there yet, but ya gotta start somewhere.

SHANIQUA SOCKWELL was sixteen when she wrote this story. She later attended college in New York City.

For more about where Shaniqua is now, see page 169.

THINK ABOUT IT

- Do you have a talent or skill that you'd like to share with others, but haven't yet? What has kept you from sharing it? What would help you share it?
- Do you have a talent or skill that you haven't really worked on or developed? What steps could you take to develop this talent or skill?

HOW I GRADUATED

by Angi Baptiste

I remember my first day of high school. I was scared and nervous, walking back and forth looking for classrooms, so confused I really wanted to cry. I think a lot of kids go through that on their first day.

It was hard at first keeping up with the classes and the teachers, especially in math. I always fell asleep in math because it was boring and I hated it. Other times I didn't care. I used to put myself down all the time. I thought I was never gonna make it. Thinking like that made me say to myself, "Why bother?"

> "It took me a while to realize that this was my future I was messing with."

It took me a while to realize that this was my future I was messing with. If other people could do it, so could I. I started to think of something someone once told me: "Never say never, until you try."

From there I decided to make a change. I started studying for every test and going over my math. When I finally made some progress in math, everything started to go well for me. I started doing my homework for every class. I knew the teachers were tired of hearing, "I left my homework on the kitchen table by mistake 'cause I was rushing for school."

The teachers were simply asking me to do my homework and classwork. That's not a hard thing to do, right? I was just lazy.

It was hard to stop being lazy. Going to math class at 8:30 in the morning wasn't my style. I would say to myself, "This week I'm gonna cut this class and that class. Next week I'll start going to all my classes." Finally, I made up my mind to stop cutting classes.

That's what my main problem was—laziness. But I knew I didn't want to get held back. I didn't want to disappoint my foster parents, because they believed I was gonna make it. That would have hurt me very much—to let them and everybody else down. Most of all, I wouldn't be proud of myself. I wouldn't be able to forgive myself for not trying hard enough.

My other problem was not being able to concentrate in school. I couldn't stop thinking about the problems I had in foster care. I couldn't stop worrying about what was going to happen to me, whether I'd be dead or alive by the age of twenty, whether I'd make it to see tomorrow.

> **"The hardest thing for me about going to school and being in foster care was when my friends would talk about their families and how cool they were. That would make me jealous, because that's not the family I have."**

But after a while I realized I had to work hard. Every time I got my report card, I knew I had to be more serious in order to reach my goals in life. To have a good future, you need a high school diploma and a college degree.

Because of my hard work, I made it to tenth grade. By then I knew everybody—every teacher and every kid in school. But I had gone back to cutting classes, although I didn't do it as often as I used to. I would only cut a class I didn't feel like going to. I didn't get back into the habit of cutting classes every day, because I would have regretted it later on.

When I started eleventh grade, I was still doing what I had to do. But in the twelfth grade, I started to panic. I was afraid I wasn't gonna make it. I couldn't concentrate in school again. I'd think about the past, about all the things I'd gone through.

A lot was on my mind. That's when I started to believe what my father used to say, that I would never graduate "because you're nothing."

Those were the thoughts on my mind 24-7. I couldn't stop worrying. I realized I needed to concentrate more when I saw my first report card from my senior year. I was disappointed with myself for thinking about other things instead of school. I wanted to do well and graduate to prove my dad wrong.

So I decided to go to night school and work extra hard. My foster parents stood by my side and got me a tutor to help me with my math three days a week. I also had tutoring in school two days a week. Boy, I started to get tired of it, but I kept going because I knew it was for the best.

The hardest thing for me about going to school and being in foster care was when my friends would talk about their families and how cool they were. That would make me jealous, because that's not the family I have. My friends would go on and on about it. Man, that used to make me so sick. It's like they would continue on about their families just to torture me. Only a few of my friends knew I was in foster care.

Hearing my friends talk about these things used to make me angry and depressed. A lot of time in class, I would be in another world, thinking about how unhappy I was with myself and my house—even though at least I wasn't living on the streets, and I thanked God for that. It's just that I wasn't happy in my foster home. So going to school was much better than being in my house. When school was over and it was time for me to go home, I would get very depressed.

School was more like my real home because everybody there cared about how I was doing. When I needed someone to talk with, the teachers were always there to listen and give me advice. The teachers cared about others too. But I got the most attention. I think the reason my teachers were always there for me was because they knew my situation and were trying to help me. I think that was very sweet of them. They wanted me to succeed.

"Never feel you're not gonna make it, because that's not true. If you work hard, everything will be okay. Just take it one day at a time. You have the power to make things happen for yourself."

After school, my social studies teacher would give me extra help. If I missed a day, I got in trouble. That showed me she cared a lot about my education. When she told me I'd passed everything, including my reading tests, and that I was graduating, I was so very happy. With God by my side, He made it happen for me.

On the day of my graduation, my foster family was there cheering for me. They were proud of me, and I was proud of myself. I made it.

The day after I graduated, I finally called my dad. I'd never kept in contact with him. When I told him I got my diploma, he cried. He wasn't expecting it. He thought I was a loser. He was expecting my sister Ingrid to graduate, but instead my sister turned out to be the dropout.

I'm angry with my sister because she gave up and stopped trying, but that doesn't mean I don't still love her. She's my big sister, and she's in my heart. She's a very big part of me.

Here's my advice to others: Never think any less of yourself because you're in foster care. Never feel you're not gonna make it, because that's not true. If you work hard, everything will be okay. Just take it one day at a time. You have the power to make things happen for yourself.

ANGI BAPTISTE was nineteen when she wrote this story.
For more about where Angi is now, see page 169.

THINK ABOUT IT

- What keeps you from succeeding? Do negative thoughts about yourself ever hold you back from doing what you need to do? What can you do to change those negative thoughts?
- Think of a time you succeeded at something, despite negative thoughts or other problems. What helped you succeed?

CREATIVITY

USING IMAGINATION

CREATIVITY is using your imagination to express yourself and to handle hurt feelings and difficult experiences.

The opposite of **CREATIVITY** is keeping your feelings bottled up inside.

CREATIVITY is hard because hurt feelings and painful experiences can weigh you down, dull your mind, and block your imagination.

CREATIVITY helps you turn something that feels ugly and bad into something beautiful. **CREATIVITY** helps you express your feelings in a positive, satisfying way.

Creativity, our fifth resilience, means using your imagination as a safe haven, a place where you're free to rearrange the details of your life as you please. Creativity is a resilience because it can help you channel overwhelming feelings and make them manageable.

When you're creative, you express yourself. You might write, dance, sing, paint, daydream, meditate, or find some other way to use your imagination. You might discover a creative way of coping with painful emotions, such as taking long walks. You might write poems and short stories. Creativity can lift the burden of reality for a little while.

You may not think of yourself as creative. But everyone has imagination. Your imagination is a rich possession that can help you see beyond what is painful or discouraging. By giving you a way to express yourself safely and productively, creativity helps you feel stronger, more hopeful, and more confident.

HOW WRITING HELPS ME

by Terry-Ann Da Costa

I think I developed a love of writing from my father. When I was a little girl, he used to sit me in his lap, hold my hand, and help me write poems and stories.

I was raised by my father on the Caribbean island of Jamaica. I started writing when I was about four years old. When I was seven, my father gave me a diary to write in so I wouldn't write on the walls or on his papers. I wrote at least three hours a day, and my father helped me whenever I wanted him to.

When I was twelve, I came to America to live with my mother. By then I was very good at writing. I wrote short stories about my family, my life, and my friends. I wrote poems about the things I was going through. If I had a bad day or a good day, I would write about what made the day so bad or so good.

"When I was seven, my father gave me a diary to write in so I wouldn't write on the walls or on his papers."

I remember that whenever I wrote a poem I would show it to my mother. She would crumple it up, throw it in the garbage, and tell me I couldn't have written it—and if I did, how did I know how to do it? When I told her that my father showed me and helped me with the poems, she would get mad and put me down.

She told me I wasn't going to be anything when I grew up, that I would only be a burger flipper. That really hurt my feelings. I couldn't understand why she was saying these things to me.

But that never stopped me from writing. I wrote about all the bad and good things she said and did to me. If she told me she loved me, I would write about how good that made me feel. If she bragged about me to her friends, I would write about how special I felt to have a mother who was not ashamed to have me for a daughter.

Soon I had five diaries filled with poems and stories.

My favorite writer is Stephen King, because I like to read and write about horror. My favorite book is *Carrie*, and my favorite poet is Edgar Allan Poe. I like Poe's poems because he writes with irony, like I do. You won't understand most of his poems if you read them only once. But if you read them over and over, you'll somehow come to understand what he's saying in your own way.

Sometimes when I'm in a bad mood and I can't think of anything to write, I choose a passage from one of my diaries and read it—or maybe I'll read all five diaries. That makes me feel better, because it's like talking to a friend.

Writing has helped me through a lot. I remember one day I was really depressed. I wrote about how I felt and what made me feel that way, and then I read over what I'd written. That helped me feel a lot better, because when I read it I couldn't believe I was capable of having those harmful, dangerous thoughts and feelings about myself.

Writing helped me when I was going through difficult times with my family—when they didn't or couldn't understand me or when they didn't understand why I would cry for no reason. Writing helped me when I needed someone to talk to. Writing is like both my friend and my family, because it's always there for me whenever I need it.

"Sometimes when I'm in a bad mood and I can't think of anything to write, I choose a passage from one of my diaries and read it. That makes me feel better, because it's like talking to a friend."

My mother still doesn't believe I can write on my own. She thinks I copy my poems and stories from someone else. My sisters think I'm crazy, because they don't see how writing words on a piece of paper could help me with my problems.

But my cousin understands me because when she was going through a difficult stage, I made her read one of my poems about the beauty of life. She said it really helped her and made her look at herself in a new way. She was also very impressed with my poems.

I would like to be a writer someday. When I publish a story or a poem, I'll give it to my mother so she can see she was wrong about me being nothing when I grow up. She'll see I can write on my own, that I didn't copy anyone's poems or stories.

She won't be able to say I'm lying, because my name will be right there on the cover.

There's another reason I would like to be a writer. I know that if someone has a problem and they read my story or poem, it might help them feel a little (or even a lot) better about themselves.

TERRY-ANN DA COSTA was sixteen when she wrote this story.

THINK ABOUT IT

- Do you ever express your thoughts and feelings in a creative way? Have you ever turned to a hobby or an activity for comfort, or to find strength?
- Have you ever used your creative talent to help another person? If so, how? If not, how do you think creativity can be used to help others?

WHY I LIVE IN A FANTASY WORLD

by Cassandra Thadal

Eyes wide open, I sit on my bed with the TV on, my pillow behind my back, surrounded by a messy book bag and papers in chaos. My mind fantasizes about singing onstage in a band with my fictional boyfriend and my friends.

Happiness grows inside us, and the crowd goes wild. Every minute someone yells, "I love you guys!" They can't resist the performance, and neither can I. I feel proud in my own world where everything is conceivable.

When I'm in my imaginary world, there are no barriers or blocks in the road. I feel free and crazy, without any doubts or worries. The world obeys me. There's no boredom, sadness, or sorrow, just fulfillment of dreams.

This fantasy world is mine, and I have no one to tell me, "You can do *that*, but not *this*." I achieve my goals, and the word *boredom* does not exist in my dictionary.

I was only about six when I began to imagine a lot. Soon I did it so much that I later nicknamed myself "Fantasy Girl."

My imagining began in small ways. On my sixth Christmas, in Haiti, my father promised to bring my sisters and brothers and me to a mall to see Santa Claus. I looked forward to going for about a week, but when we finally got there, we found no Santa Claus. My father had misunderstood the date. I felt so bad, but then I imagined what I didn't get. During the night, I pictured that Santa Claus brought me hundreds of presents.

"When I'm in my imaginary world, there are no barriers or blocks in the road. I feel free and crazy, without any doubts or worries."

My relatives and friends don't know I'm a dreamer. Sometimes I think I'm the only one who imagines for so many hours. I don't mind that I spend a lot of my life in an imaginary place, but I'm scared that people would think I was crazy if they knew.

I imagine to improve my life. When problems come without solutions, and dreams and desires are impossible to accomplish, I dream the opposite to keep myself from getting depressed.

Imagination also helps me get through the chores I dislike and gives me something to do during my moments of boredom. Lots of times, I imagine just for amusement and to keep my mind busy.

Sometimes as I lean on the subway train's doors, instead of looking at people, I fancy my future. In my mind, I'm a healthy, beautiful woman who lives in Florida or in the West Indies. I'm a famous journalist and clothing designer.

My children spend a lot of time with me, and I always help them do their homework. I have a wonderful husband and a nice, simple family. I imagine that I make about $30,000 every week, and that I spend half my money on poor people to give them the chance to be happy.

Helping poor people is my dream because I hate pain, either physical or emotional. Knowing that a lot of kids in this world are suffering hurts me.

"Sometimes my imagination is pure fantasy, but in other ways it helps me in my real life. Imagining situations gets me ready to confront the people I don't enjoy talking to."

Doing something I dislike, such as washing dishes, always makes me fantasize about my future boyfriend. While I scrub the dirty, half-burned pans and the warm water and soapy liquid flows through my fingers, I picture him, the imaginary person I'll love. My boyfriend is very charming and cute and he loves only me, not for what I look like but for what's inside me. We shine in each other's lives and are two in one.

Often, we sit side by side near the ocean and talk. We study together, play jokes on each other, and play all the time. I don't know his name, but I'm sure we're like two little kids, knowing only good and sharing a love too perfect and strong to be defined.

Sometimes my imagination is pure fantasy, but in other ways it helps me in my real life. Imagining situations gets me ready to confront the people I don't enjoy talking to.

For instance, I live with my aunts, and I know they'll have lots of questions whenever I ask to do anything late at night. To prepare myself to talk to them, I imagine a short conversation between us. Once when I wanted to go to a school festival one night, I was worried my aunt wouldn't let me go.

"I'm going to my school festival," I imagined myself saying.

"Of course you have to go. What time does it start?" she said in my head.

Fortunately, that time she really did give me permission without asking lots of questions.

People rarely know that my body is in this world while my mind is elsewhere, but when I'm caught imagining, it seems as if people believe I have a mental disorder by the way they stare at me.

After school one day, I was heading to the subway station and imagining my older brother chasing after me for being sassy. I made gestures as I visualized the scene.

Suddenly a staff member from my school stopped me.

"Why are you talking to yourself?" he said.

"How do you know I was talking to myself?" I said.

"I could see that," he answered. To my great relief, he changed the subject.

Another time, I was going to Boston on the bus. I imagined I was lost in a castle. In my mind I climbed hundreds of stairs as I admired the walls full of pictures of a royal family. I walked in the castle for three hours and still hadn't found anyone.

Tired, I thought there was no end to the stairs. Then a giant man stepped out and scared me. He told me a long story about the royal family who lived in the castle and how they would die if they left their rooms. The story went like this:

"When I'm caught imagining, it seems as if people believe I have a mental disorder by the way they stare at me."

"One day the king and queen had a son. But the prince was disrespectful and spoiled. At fourteen, he hated his father's generosity and paid a wizard to turn the king into a cruel and selfish man.

"After that, the king never helped his people. One year later, another wizard snuck into the castle and begged for some food. The king refused, so the wizard sentenced him, saying, 'You will never have another generation because the prince is now a dog and you cannot run away. The only way for all this to change is if a poor lady agrees to marry that dog.'

"'Oh, that's so sad,' I said.

"'Please, beautiful lady, you have to marry the dog and teach it to love.'

"'Yes, I will marry the dog,' I said."

I opened my eyes with the man's voice in my thoughts and started laughing about marrying a dog. My chest went up and down, and I couldn't stop.

The man sitting next to me on the bus said, "What's wrong with you, girl? I'm trying to sleep."

I ignored the man and tried to stop laughing, but that was impossible, so I went to finish in the restroom. As I went, my hands over my mouth, laughing not at the dream anymore but at the man sitting next to me, some people stared at me. Living in an imaginary world sometimes causes bad results in the real world.

"Though I imagine, I also work for my dreams in the present. It's good to imagine your goals so you have a picture of them and can believe in yourself."

And sometimes I do get really tired of imagining. I get nervous because I live so much in my imagination, dreaming of things that can't be realities. But overall, imagination has more good than bad effects on me. Being a fantasy girl helps me live my dreams instead of dwelling on what I don't have.

Though I imagine, I also work for my dreams in the present. It's good to imagine your goals so you have a picture of them and can believe in yourself. You can look ahead at your "wished for" future. You can say, "If I imagine it, then I can be it."

Imagination doesn't solve my problems, but it helps me find and follow the road to my goals. I find my happiness in my imagination, because that's where the impossible things in our normal lives become possible.

CASSANDRA THADAL was fifteen when she wrote this story.

THINK ABOUT IT

- What role does imagination play in your life? Does it help you deal with difficult situations or feelings? If so, how?
- Can creativity and imagination ever be harmful? Why or why not?

WALKING OUT THE ANGER

by Tamara Ballard

As a teenager, I'm entitled to my moods. However, my moods can become stressful at times, especially when I don't know what causes them to change. My mood swings are predictable, but not controllable. I can be extremely energetic and hyper for about an hour, then be totally sad and down for the next three days or so. There are days when I'm calm, but those days don't come along too often.

On the days when I'm really moody, I don't like to be around people. If I have to talk to people I will, for no apparent reason, snap at them. I snap at everybody: teachers, other adults, and peers. I'm truly snotty around this time.

If I'm moody on a day I have school, most likely I will cut and go to the most relaxing and quiet place I know that opens early in the morning. That's right, readers—I take a one-hour-and-forty-five-minute ride to my "hideaway": Coney Island.

It may be hard to believe, but Coney Island is actually peaceful. I sit there and I watch the birds fly, the waves roll in, the people run along the boardwalk for exercise. If I get there early enough, I can watch the tide go from high to low. It's amazing how the large rocks appear from the tide going low.

> "My mood swings are predictable, but not controllable."

Coney Island helps me think clearly. It's the only place where I can think without someone calling my name every five minutes. At Coney Island there are no phones ringing, no teachers screaming, no kids crying. The list goes on.

On weekends, when I don't feel like getting out of bed, I'll sometimes try to sleep my attitude off. But at home there's always something that disrupts my sleep. That's when I'll take a walk.

I'm not talking about a walk around the block either. I'm talking about walking from one part of the city to another.

One particular day, I hadn't planned on walking. My friend Anthony had invited me to hang out. Since I had nothing better to do, I said yeah. But when I arrived, he wasn't there. (I found out later that his job had called him in at the last moment.)

I wasn't in the mood to return home so early. And there was some personal stuff I wanted to think about, some anger I needed to get out of my system. (I'd recently had an argument with someone over stupid stuff.)

So I had two choices—I could ride the trains to no place in particular, or I could walk to my sister's job. I decided to walk from 22nd Street and First Avenue in Manhattan to 92nd Street and Lexington Avenue. I walked seventy whole blocks, not including the blocks to get from First Avenue to Lexington. From all that walking, I was calm by the time I reached my sister's job.

"Walking helps me burn off some of my negative emotions. It takes that adrenaline rush to hate and fight and does something good with it. Walking also helps me clear my head. I walk until I can't walk anymore."

(Did I mention that if it hadn't been so dark when I got there, I would have walked all the way home, which is in the Bronx on East Tremont and Belmont?)

Another time when I felt stressed, I walked from Hempstead Transit (a bus terminal in Hempstead, Long Island) to 179th Street in Queens. I couldn't tell you how many blocks that is. But it takes forty-five minutes to an hour by bus, so come to your own conclusions.

Many times, I've walked from 151st Street and Eighth Avenue in Manhattan to Third Avenue in the Bronx. Or, when I have to do hair on my old block, I walk to Ms. Barbara's house. This means walking from East Tremont and Belmont back to 151st Street and Eighth Avenue.

Walking helps me burn off some of my negative emotions. It takes that adrenaline rush to hate and fight and does something good with it. Walking also helps me clear my head. I walk until I can't walk anymore. I don't stop walking because I'm tired. I stop because I reach my destination or because it's too dark to walk.

But walking and going to Coney Island aren't the only ways I release stress and anger. I also write. Many people say the way to get to know me is to read my poetry, because when I talk to people there's a lot left out.

I don't usually feel comfortable talking about my real feelings. I've gotten so used to wearing what I call a "happy mask." For those of you who don't know me personally, a "happy mask" is when I put on a fake smile all day. Or at least until I get around someone I can be real with.

Writing is so easy for me because I can be as real as I want to be and not have to worry about being judged because of how I feel. I've written about forty poems. I write about love, hate, happiness, sadness, life, death, and friendship.

Sometimes writing poetry is hard, so I write stories. Whether they're fiction or nonfiction, writing stories helps me. I write about everyday stuff.

I recently wrote a story about what happened between me and my first love. I added scenes and a happy ending to fit my desires. But in real life it wasn't so happy. That story was a blend of fiction and nonfiction. My first love thought popularity was everything. His attitude toward things put a real strain on our relationship. When we were on school grounds, he acted real snotty because he had an image to protect.

"Writing is so easy for me because I can be as real as I want to be and not have to worry about being judged because of how I feel."

One day I'll put my journal and stories together. When I get older, they'll make the perfect autobiography. I started my first journal a few years ago. It's fun to look at my old journal and see how much I've matured.

Relieving stress is something I must do to stay centered. Writing and walking are two things that help me. But Coney Island has proved to be the best for me. All I need is to get away. And Coney Island is as far as I can go without being considered a runaway.

TAMARA BALLARD was sixteen when she wrote this story. She later lived in Augusta, Georgia, where she was an honors student in high school and played volleyball. Tamara also wrote "She's My Sister (Not Foster)," (page 66).

THINK ABOUT IT

- What activities help you cope with stress, anger, or depression? What's your favorite activity? Why is it your favorite?
- Why do you think expressing your feelings through an activity or creative outlet is sometimes easier than talking about them?

HUMOR

FINDING WHAT'S FUNNY

HUMOR is finding what's funny, even when you're sad or in pain.

The opposite of **HUMOR** is taking yourself and your situation too seriously.

HUMOR is hard because pressures can blot out the lighter side of life.

HUMOR helps you put pain in perspective. **HUMOR** helps you laugh and let others laugh with you.

Humor, our sixth resilience, allows you to find what's funny in what seems sad, tragic, stressful, or just embarrassing. Instead of taking yourself and your situation too seriously, you use humor to see the lighter side. Humor—laughter—is a resilience because it's a wonderful way to release tension and to relieve pain or embarrassment.

There may be times when you don't see any humor in your situation. The reality seems too grim, boring, or stressful. But, like creativity, humor lets you find a positive way to respond to difficult situations. Humor gives you a healthy perspective on your life and lets you see beyond what's happening right now. As you'll see in the following stories, a sense of humor is a precious gift.

MY HAIR IS BLUE— BUT I'M NOT A FREAK!

by Lenny Jones

My whole life (all 192 months), I've been teased about the size of my head. When I was in elementary school, a group of kids would march around me in the schoolyard during lunch singing "big head and little body" over and over again.

Now that I'm in high school, the teasing still goes on. Sometimes people call me cartoon character names. It's not my fault that I have a so-called "big head" (I see nothing wrong with the size of it). I try to flush these things out of my system, but they always come back.

To stop the name-calling, I thought I'd wear my hat in school. But sexist teachers told me to take it off or else they would suspend me. (They're sexist because they let girls, but not guys, wear hats in school.)

So, if I couldn't wear a hat, I decided I would get back at the teachers and the kids who teased me in a way they'd never forget. I would hit them where it hurt the most—in their eyes.

"I decided to dye my hair platinum white. I hoped to distract people from making fun of my head and send all the attention to my hair."

I decided to dye my hair platinum white *(ahhh!—the horror)*. I hoped to distract people from making fun of my head and send all the attention to my hair.

When I told someone I knew about my hair-dyeing plans, she thought I was crazy. (I was not only going to dye my hair, but also get a perm to make my hair straight and a blowout to make it puffy, all in one weekend.) She said I would end up having bald spots, my head would be burning, etc.

So instead, I asked her to do the dyeing for me. She was hesitant at first, but finally she said okay.

I went to a drugstore with my friend to find the hair coloring. We looked all around the store but couldn't find a color to my liking. Then we found this hair color matching system (it's like a computer program that helps you find the right coloring product).

Well, the program wasn't much help, but it had a toll-free number to call. I called and told the hair specialist what shade I was looking for. She told me to buy the Always Been Blonde hair lightener kit. She said to buy two kits so my hair would come out a pale, pale blond (like the inside of a banana). So I took her advice, although I wanted my hair even whiter than that.

It took about three or four days of running from store to store to find the kit. It cost ten dollars and change, but I didn't care. (Too bad I only had enough for one kit—what do you expect with this penny-per-hour job of mine?)

> **"As I was going home, my heart started beating faster and faster. I knew that the next day my life would change."**

As I was going home, my heart started beating faster and faster. I knew that the next day my life would change. That night I called all my friends (both of them) and told them I was going to dye my hair. They cheered me on and gave me more confidence.

The next evening, my friend mixed the solution together and put it into my hair. As soon as I felt the stuff on my scalp, I got mad nervous. My friend kept saying, "Keep your eyes closed." The stuff started tingling and burning. I got more and more nervous. It felt like my hair was falling out, but my friend assured me it wasn't. Ten minutes later she wiped my face and told me to open my eyes, but I was too scared.

She told me to calm down and open my eyes. So I finally did. She told me my hair was already changing color and to go look in the mirror. To my surprise, she was right. It was turning brass-brown. I still wanted it white. I was supposed to leave the stuff in for two hours, but I kept it in for three. (I would have left it in longer, but everybody told me, "Take it out before your hair falls out.")

So my friend washed it out for me and put in a conditioner. After that, I dried it off.

Unfortunately, it didn't come out platinum white, but yellow!

I thought after I dyed my hair, people would stop making fun of me (and, besides that, I wanted something different). In some ways it worked, but it also backfired.

For instance, the first day I went to school, everyone laughed (at least they didn't laugh at the size of my head), which hurt a lot (thank God there's only about 250 students in my school). But later I got a few apologies. Some of the girls told me they liked it and I should keep it that way.

People still called me names, but I felt much more comfortable with them. I didn't mind them as much. Some of the more creative names were "Sunny," "Nacho Cheesehead," "The Golden Child," "Tweety Bird," "Blondy," and "Gold Fro."

But some people hated it. One of the teachers said she wanted me to change my hair back because she only liked "real" brothers. Yet she had the nerve to come to school with some old, nappy, fake dreadlocks that she stripped from a poor, defenseless mop!

"I thought after I dyed my hair, people would stop making fun of me (and, besides that, I wanted something different). In some ways it worked, but it also backfired."

Some thought my new hair color made me look gay. Some comments were, "That look mad gay," "Stay black!" and "Wash that stuff out of your hair!"

The comments didn't apply to me, so I just made jokes. I'd say, "I'm going through that Michael Jackson stage. I woke up one morning, and my hair was in blotches of bright blondish-yellow. I just had to lighten all my hair to match it."

Some of them believed me! I also joked about dyeing my hair white, then buying those cans of spray-on hair coloring.

One girl said I hurt her when I dyed my hair because she had a crush on me. I told her that if she didn't like my hair, she didn't like me. She said she still liked me but was prejudiced against my hair. It hurt *me* to see all those naps up in her hair (if that's what she wants to call it), but did I complain to her? (Nooo!)

When people said I wasn't keepin' it real, I asked them if they ever dyed their hair. They said yeah. Then they realized how stupid they sounded and just changed the subject.

After about two months of having my hair yellow, I dyed it several shades of blue. Now they started calling me "Little Boy Blue," "Blue Dandruff," "The Blue Ranger" (from that show *Power Rangers*), and "Papa Smurf" (or just plain "Smurf").

The principal wanted me to try a more "conservative" style. He told me to leave my hair blue and dye two white lightning bolts across it. Then he said I should wear some crazy-looking shorts and mismatched stockings. (Where do they get these people?)

The assistant principal wanted me to color one side red and one side green and wear bells so I could be her "mobile Christmas tree." (Yeah, right!)

Some people wanted me to dye my hair red, green, and even fuchsia (yikes!).

Eventually I took the blue out of my hair. Soon I'm going to dye it jet-black. Once I do that, I'm probably going to braid or twist it. Then I'll leave it alone for a while.

LENNY JONES was sixteen when he wrote this story. He later attended college in Manhattan.

THINK ABOUT IT

- Have you ever been teased? Have you ever felt self-conscious about your appearance? If so, how did that feel? What did you do about it?
- Have you ever wanted to change your appearance? In what way? If you did change your appearance, how did the change affect the way you felt about yourself?

HOW TO SURVIVE SHOPPING WITH MOM

by Chris Kanarick

It's Saturday. You and your friends decide to go clothes shopping. Before leaving, you explain your plans to Mom, who's confused.

"You have $5,000 worth of clothes sitting in your room," she says. (Mothers tend to exaggerate quite a bit.) "You mean to tell me that none of the stuff from last year fits you?"

There are a few possible answers to this question:

A) "It fits, but my little brother likes it. So being the kind-hearted person I am . . ."

B) "Mom, if I don't buy new clothes, those guys in the mall who work on commission won't make any money to support their families, and their children will die a slow, horrible death. Do you really want that on your conscience?"

C) "That's right. None of it fits."

Needless to say, C is usually the most popular choice.

"Why don't I come with you?" she asks. Your first impulse is, "Oh, no!" But think for a minute. Mom's got the credit cards.

You call up your friends and tell them you can't go. "Mom got you, huh?" they'll reply sympathetically.

So, you and Mom pile into the ol' family car and you're on your merry way to the mall. On the way there, Mom will tell you that she doesn't have much time to waste because she's got (INSERT NAME OF MEAT HERE) in the oven.

Next, she will tell you that she doesn't have much money, so she's not going to spend $10,000 (there's that exaggeration thing again) on clothes that you won't be able to wear again next year, anyway. She'll explain what your brother or sister bought and how much it cost, just so you have an idea of what to look forward to.

> **So, you and Mom pile into the ol' family car and you're on your merry way to the mall."**

As you and Mom begin your leisurely stroll through the first floor of the mall, Mom will suddenly veer off to the left, arms outstretched, eyes wide, nose in the air, looking like something out of a zombie movie. Mothers can smell a sale from a mile away. There is no scientific explanation for this—it just happens. Follow her. You have no choice. Remember who's got the money.

Mom will stop and explain that your aunt's friend's cousin has a roommate who has a brother who thinks this store "is the greatest thing since sliced bread," whatever that means. Without waiting for a response, she heads toward the rack marked "50 PERCENT OFF."

After you find fault with every item Mom picks out, you explain that since you went to her store, now she can go to yours. If nothing else, mothers are fair. Pick the most expensive store in the mall and lead the way.

Once you get there, Mom will go off in her own direction, as usual. You'll pick out several items that she disapproves of—except for one shirt, which she complains about anyway.

"Mothers can smell a sale from a mile away. There is no scientific explanation for this—it just happens. Follow her. You have no choice. Remember who's got the money."

"Twenty dollars for a shirt?" she'll say. "You'd think it was made out of gold!" She may tell you that she saw the same item in the other store for half-price. There's no way out of this one, so don't even try it.

After circling the mall a few times, with several stops along the way, Mom will decide to head for one final store—a favorite among women, a last resort among men—the mother of all department stores . . . Macy's.

Mom will immediately head to the boys' department. One of the other major problems with mothers is they forget that although they do give birth to a baby, it usually doesn't stay that small.

Set her straight. Explain that you belong in the men's department (although I think Macy's has a teen department for those of us who haven't got a clue what size we wear).

This will make her nostalgic, and she'll tell you how big her baby is getting—you know the deal.

Mothers come equipped with a built-in tracking system. Somehow, they always manage to find someone they know at

Macy's. Mom will talk to her friend while you pick up several items. When you turn to show them to her, she's already behind you, holding up a shirt with little red and pink flowers on it.

"This is spiffy," she says. You recall a discussion you had recently about a flowered shirt in which your friend explained that if he wore it, "I'd be mocked, I'd be jeered at." "You'd be watered," you replied. The *Magnum, P.I.* reject goes back on the rack.

Trying on clothes can be a nightmare in itself. You put on a pair of jeans and they feel pretty comfortable—a little long, but that can be taken care of. So you go out to get Mom's opinion.

"How do they feel?" she asks. You tell her they feel fine. Next, she'll want you to walk around in them. So now you're walking barefoot around the Macy's teen department in a pair of jeans you don't even own. Not too awkward, right?

"Just remember, you're not alone in this crazy, mixed-up world where mothers reign supreme. Someday, you'll be able to stand tall like me and say: 'Hi, my name is Chris, and I've gone shopping with my mother.'"

She'll ask you to squat. Then she'll start getting personal. "How do they feel in the crotch?" "Ma!" you exclaim. "Not so loud! They feel fine."

The next thing you know, she thrusts her fingers into your pants and is running them along your waist to make sure there isn't "enough room for three more people in there," as she puts it.

Now, some of you may be laughing at me and saying, "Oh, I don't know what you're talking about." But there are others—you know who you are. Just remember, you're not alone in this crazy, mixed-up world where mothers reign supreme. Someday, you'll be able to stand tall like me and say: "Hi, my name is Chris, and I've gone shopping with my mother."

CHRIS KANARICK was seventeen when he wrote this story. He lived with his mom (and shopped with her) on Staten Island.

For more about where Chris is now, see page 169.

THINK ABOUT IT

- Have you ever used humor to make the best of an unpleasant situation? How well did it work? Did your view of the situation change as a result?
- If you were a parent, how would you handle clothes shopping with your teenager?

MORALITY

DOING THE RIGHT THING

MORALITY is thinking of others as well as yourself. It's learning what other people need and trying to give it to them.

The opposite of **MORALITY** is thinking only of yourself, or doing whatever suits you or whatever you can get away with.

MORALITY is hard because it can mean sacrificing your own best or short-term interests to do what's right for other people.

MORALITY helps connect you to other people through being useful and caring. **MORALITY** helps you feel you're a good person.

Morality, our seventh resilience, means doing the *right* thing, even if it's not the easy or natural thing. When you're a moral person you learn what other people need and you try to give it to them. You're able to see that others struggle, hope, and dream just as you do. You remember and do what's decent and fair even when it's easier not to. You work to change the painful conditions in the world. Morality is a resilience because it prevents you from becoming cynical or giving up on the world and its potential for beauty, even when your personal life has gone dark.

Teenagers are not often recognized for their morality. We usually hear that kids are thoughtless, disrespectful, only interested in themselves and their own pleasures. If we hear about the morality of teens at all, it's usually in a story about a service project that was a graduation requirement or a "superkid" who's almost too good to be true.

In a book called *The Moral Life of Children* (Boston: Atlantic Monthly Press, 2000), the psychiatrist Robert Coles writes about children who live in some of the most difficult places in the world, but who value and act with compassion, fairness, and decency. These children give what they were never given. They believe they can make better lives for themselves in the future by doing what's right in the present. Their morality lifts them above their harsh circumstances.

Morality encourages you to see the strength that is possible in human nature. All the writers in this section have learned to reach out to others in need. That reaching out has made them stronger themselves.

A MOTHER TO MY MOTHER'S CHILDREN

by Charlene Johnson

Many teenagers choose to become parents. I didn't have that choice. By the age of twelve I was raising my brother and four sisters with only a little help from my mother.

It all started when my mother began to use drugs. She was unable to take care of my brother and sisters, so she put me in charge. Well, I actually put myself in charge, because my siblings were beginning to go wild.

When my brother and sisters found out I was in command, they began to act crazy. They thought they would be staying home from school and watching TV all day, but they soon found out I wasn't having that.

"It all started when my mother began to use drugs. She was unable to take care of my brother and sisters, so she put me in charge."

Every morning I made sure my eleven-year-old brother, Anthony, got on the bus and went to school. Then I walked my eight- and nine-year-old sisters, Charmel and Charisse, to school. When I came back home, I'd find my twin sister, Charlotte, still sleeping.

It was hard for me to be in charge of Charlotte, because although we were the same age, she felt she was older than me just because she was born four minutes earlier. But I made sure she went to school with me, even though we went late most of the time.

I never stayed in school for a full day because I had to pick up my little sisters from school, and then my brother from the bus stop. If I didn't pick Anthony up, he'd wander off somewhere and wouldn't be found until late at night.

The worst times were when everyone was home after school and during the weekends. My brother and sisters would fight and argue constantly. And my mother couldn't care less because she was so high on drugs most of the time that she didn't know what was going on.

My mother was in no shape to take care of us. She was locked up in her room when she was home, and most of the time she wasn't even there. She would either be at her friend's house or in some crack house.

I tried to make my brother and sisters stop arguing by telling them to go out and get some air, but then they would fight people outside. I knew it wasn't right, but at the time I liked to see them beat someone up. It made me feel good to see they could stand up for themselves. I just didn't like it when they fought each other.

Except for the fighting and arguing, my siblings listened to what I told them to do. They knew what time to be home and that they had to do their homework before going outside. They always wore clean clothes, took baths (when I told them to), and did little things around the house (but only when they saw I was about to get tired and aggravated from doing everything myself all the time).

After a while, I started to get used to being the mother of the house.

Sometimes my mother would get sick and I'd have to take care of her. I had a feeling she was jealous of me because she'd say, "May I please go out, Mother?" After she said it, she'd laugh at me.

Then my mother had another baby. When she first told me she was pregnant, I wanted to strangle her. I couldn't believe she was having another child when she couldn't even take care of the babies she already had.

"After a while, I started to get used to being the mother of the house."

My mother stopped taking drugs when she was pregnant and for two months after she gave birth to Baby Troy. I thought that my "mother days" were over, that I would be able to go to school again and have a normal teenage life. But my mother slowly started to put Baby Troy on me too.

Late one night, I heard Baby Troy crying. The next thing I knew, my mother gave me his bottle, laid him beside me, and told me she'd be back the next morning. I was about to argue with her, but it seemed useless.

The next day I knew I would have to be a mother all over again. But it was going to be harder because Baby Troy was only three months old.

I had no idea how to take care of a baby. I wasn't quite fourteen, and I had a whole family to take care of! But all I really had to worry about at that point was the baby, because Charlotte helped take care of the others.

At first I loved to be with Baby Troy. I acted like his mother, and I think he thought I was. I did everything except breastfeed. He was the reason I continued to be strong and didn't have a mental breakdown. I felt I was the only person he had, and that if I failed him, he would have no one else.

But I started to dislike it a little when he began to get teeth. Remember, I wasn't even fourteen and didn't know anything about babies except the basic stuff, like making a bottle or changing diapers.

One day I took Baby Troy out and we had a good time, but when we returned home he wouldn't stop crying. I did everything to make him quiet. I changed his diapers, I gave him toys, I tried to feed him, but nothing worked.

"At first I loved to be with Baby Troy. I acted like his mother, and I think he thought I was."

Then my mother came out of her room with some ointment and told me to put some on his gums. I did, and he stopped crying instantly. The ointment numbed his gums so he couldn't feel the pain of his teeth coming through. I was so happy, and so was Baby Troy. He went straight to sleep and didn't wake up 'til the next morning.

If my mother hadn't come out with the ointment and told me what to do, I think I would have done something to Baby Troy that I probably would have regretted for the rest of my life. I realize now that parents sometimes hit their children because they get so stressed out and don't know what else to do.

The drugs my mother was using started to affect her really badly. She got sick and had to go to the hospital.

I thought this was my time to get away for a while and have some fun, so Charlotte and I ran away. I didn't worry about the other kids because I thought a relative had everything under control.

We stayed away for three weeks and came home to find the children gone. My mother was high as the sky and acting really snotty. I asked where the kids were and she didn't answer. All she did was say nasty things and try to argue with us.

Finally I found out they were at my aunt's house. I was so relieved to hear that. I thought my mother had given them away or something.

When my brothers and sisters got home, they were so happy to see me. Baby Troy ran up to me and stayed with me for the rest of the time we were together. My mother didn't like that Baby Troy thought I was his mother. But it was her fault—she should have taken care of her responsibilities. Then she could have had her son.

After two weeks I was placed in foster care. I still came back home and watched Baby Troy and the other kids. My mother was going to a rehab program so my other siblings could stay with her.

> **"When I do have children, I will take care of them until they can take care of themselves."**

But my mother never fully accomplished her goal, and none of her kids now live with her. Anthony lives with my aunt. Baby Troy lives with his father's family. Charmel and Charisse live in one foster home, and Charlotte and I live in another foster home.

I try to keep in contact with all my siblings, except Baby Troy. I don't like to see him because when I do, I don't want to leave. I love him so much and I hate to be away from him, so that's why I keep my distance.

Baby Troy has made me change my mind about having children. I always said to myself that I would never have kids of my own, but after being with him I do want kids. I want to give a child the love and joy I gave Baby Troy when I was taking care of him. When I do have children, I will take care of them until they can take care of themselves.

I don't know how a mother could have children and not do everything in her power to keep them. I wasn't a birth mother but I was very close to it, and I think sometimes that I lost my children instead of my brothers and sisters.

A good number of foster children have had experiences like mine. I want to say to them—don't look at your troubles in a bad way. Try to think of them as temporary setbacks that have made you a stronger person.

I know my experiences have made me stronger. Looking after my brothers and sisters has made me feel I have the power to overcome any obstacle that comes my way.

People say children are products of their environment. Well, I am not. I am not going to follow in my mother's footsteps and have seven children and not be able to be part of their lives. I'm going to be the best parent I can be. As long as I get a good education and career, I'll be able to give my children what they need and what they deserve.

But more than anything, I will love and care for them until the day I die.

CHARLENE JOHNSON was seventeen when she wrote this story. She is also the author of "My Weight Is No Burden" (page 40).

THINK ABOUT IT

- Have you ever had to take responsibility for someone or something that really was not your responsibility? How did that feel? Looking back, would you do it again? Why or why not?
- What does "doing the right thing" mean to you? How does it apply to your life? What's the difference between "doing the right thing" and taking on too much responsibility?

NO ONE SPOKE UP FOR IRMA

by Ana Angélica Pines

They say if you look into someone's eyes you can see their soul. When I look into my friend Irma's eyes, I see reflections of the past. We're around five or six years old, and we're crossing the street on the way to the fruit market. Suddenly the cart Irma's mother, Carmen, is pushing tips over, and her groceries fall out in the middle of the street. She grabs Irma's head and bangs it against the handlebar of the cart. Irma is bleeding from her lip now, and both she and her younger sister Lydia are crying as we all help pick the stuff up off the ground.

The next thing I know, my mother, my sister, and I are walking away as if nothing has happened. Lydia comes running after us and grabs onto my mother's leg. "Don't let her hit *me*!" she screams.

Carmen comes over, takes Lydia by the arm, and pulls her back across the street to where Irma is standing, still in tears. As we walk away, nobody says a word. To this day, I still don't know what to think about that moment.

> "Everyone on the block saw what was going on, but no one ever did anything to stop it. As far as I could see, the kids were the only ones who ever confronted Carmen about what she was doing."

Irma is sixteen now. The two of us grew up together in the same building. Ever since we were little, Irma's mother would hit her, throw things at her, and curse her. She would buy Lydia things and take her places, but she always ignored Irma and made her stay behind.

Everyone on the block saw what was going on, but no one ever did anything to stop it. As far as I could see, the kids were the only ones who ever confronted Carmen about what she was doing. We quickly got the message, however, that if we kept it up we'd get in trouble. As long as they made us stay quiet, the adults could pretend the problem didn't exist.

For some reason, Carmen always favored Lydia over Irma. Even if the two girls did the same thing, only Irma would get in trouble. When Irma turned five, for example, there was a joint birthday party for her and her older brother. Lydia didn't want food, she wanted candy, so she threw her food away. Irma saw this and did the same.

Carmen grabbed Irma and slapped her right in front of everybody (and on her birthday). Then she forced her to eat all the food on her plate (too much to give a little girl in the first place). My sister fed it to her while wiping her tears, and we put some on my plate when Carmen wasn't looking.

"Irma was never allowed to go out either. Anytime we asked if she could go someplace with us, we were told she was being punished or she just couldn't go."

Carmen's abuse wasn't always physical, however. On Christmas morning Irma's siblings would still be opening their presents long after Irma had finished. Every fall she and her sister would get jeans and some shirts to start off the school year. But as the year progressed, Lydia's wardrobe would continue to grow, while Irma's stayed the same. All through junior high school she wore the same thing every week.

Irma was never allowed to go out either. Anytime we asked if she could go someplace with us, we were told she was being punished or she just couldn't go.

Once when we were around seven or eight, Peter, one of the kids from the block, had the guts to go up to Carmen and ask her, "Why can Lydia come downstairs and not Irma?"

Not long after that, a girl named Melissa decided to go up to Carmen and tell her to her face: "You're a child abuser!" Carmen got really mad, and I remember thinking to myself, "She knows she is."

When they heard about what happened, both Peter's mother and Melissa's mother told them the same thing: "Mind your own business."

After I turned seven or eight, I hardly ever went to Irma and Lydia's house; I couldn't stand to watch it anymore. But my sister was always over there—she was practically a member of the family. Irma always had to fold everybody's laundry, sweep and mop, and basically clean the whole house. When Carmen wasn't there, my sister would help her.

Other times, my sister would grab Carmen when she was about to hit Irma and take her outside for a walk to calm her down. I often wonder how many more beatings Irma would have gotten if it hadn't been for my sister.

But most of the neighbors just accepted the situation. In fact, they used to favor Lydia just as much as Carmen did. They'd give her better presents at Christmas and take her to the beach and to the country in the summertime. Irma always had to stay home. At times my family took Lydia places too. After all, it wasn't her fault. She was just a child herself.

One summer, Lydia got to go visit relatives in Florida. Once again Irma was going to have to stay home. My family was going to Guatemala, and my mother offered to take her with us.

"I'm not giving her anything," said Carmen.

"Fine, I'll pay for everything," my mother told her. But we ended up not taking Irma because it was too late to get her a passport.

When Irma turned sixteen her mother wasn't planning to do anything for her—not even dinner. So my family decided to throw her our own surprise party at my cousin's house. We had *pernil* (roast pork), *arroz con gandules* (rice with chickpeas), and a big cake. There were *kapias* (souvenir pins) and *recuerdos* (little ceramic figurines) for people to take home, and we took lots of pictures.

The funny thing was that Irma didn't even know half the people there. Nobody from her family came. When we told Carmen about the party she said, "No one from this house is going."

Since the people who did come knew about Irma's situation, they all chipped in and even bought her gifts. It was awkward, but Irma enjoyed it. When Carmen found out, however, she got mad and started crying. Lydia always had *piñatas*, candy, and presents on her birthday. When Lydia turns sixteen next year, Carmen is planning a big ceremony with the *damas* and *caballeros* (girls in fancy dresses, guys in tuxedos) and everything. But for some reason, Carmen doesn't want Irma to have anything in life.

"For some reason, Carmen doesn't want Irma to have anything in life."

About a year ago, my mother offered to adopt Irma. She told Carmen that if she didn't want her, Irma could come live with us. But Carmen made excuses, saying Irma was lazy and stupid and that she didn't want us to have to put up with her. When she saw my mother was serious, she just told her no and walked out.

When somebody tells you something often enough, sooner or later you begin to believe it. For example, back when we were younger, Lydia, many of the other girls on the block, and I all used to go to dancing school. Irma stayed home and did chores. Her mother's excuse was that Irma wasn't any good at dance and didn't like it. She repeated it so many times that Irma eventually agreed with her.

Irma's family always told her she was worthless, that she'd never do anything in life but get married, have kids, and cook eggs all day. She says worthless is how she now feels and "that's what they expect, so that's what I'm going to give them."

"When somebody tells you something often enough, sooner or later you begin to believe it."

Lately, Irma's been doing very badly in school. She cuts all the time and failed every class but one last semester. She gets into fights a lot and always wears baggy jeans and the same shirt. She hardly ever wears makeup, and she talks like a hoodlum.

A couple of years ago she was in the hospital. She told my sister that she wished she'd died so she would never have to go back to that house again.

I try to make things appealing to her so she'll want to do better. "If you're sick of your house, go to school," I tell her. "Then you can graduate on time and move out, go to college, or get a job. You can even move in with me."

It's strange, because even though Irma grew up with nothing, she still turned out superficial and ditzy. She's only interested in name-brand clothing, and if she gets any money she blows it on sneakers.

These days Irma always has this blank look on her face—like there's nothing there. It's like looking into space. It's scary. She's so lost and seems to have no sense of direction.

In June, my sister and I were on the train with Irma and noticed she had carved her name in her arm with a needle. We asked her why, and she said it was because she wanted to feel pain.

I guess pain is what she's used to feeling. I don't know. I don't understand how she thinks. Sometimes I can't help but ask myself, "Why is she so stupid?" But then I think about the way she's always been told how worthless she is.

"So many people saw the pain Irma suffered and stayed quiet. Everyone in that building knew what was going on. We all did little things to make Irma feel better, but no one ever really spoke up or tried to get her out of the situation."

Don't get me wrong—Irma has a lot of friends and people like her. But what good are friends if you don't like yourself? Sometimes I wish I could just hold her and tell her that everything is going to be okay. I wish I could predict the future, but I can't. The only thing that can be done now is for her to get help.

So many people saw the pain Irma suffered and stayed quiet. Everyone in that building knew what was going on. We all did little things to make Irma feel better, but no one ever really spoke up or tried to get her out of the situation.

When I was little I thought a lot about calling those hotlines for abused children, but I was always afraid they would somehow be able to figure out who I was. I thought maybe they'd blow me off because I was only a child, and then not do anything anyway. Not many of the adults I knew listened to children.

But what if they did show up at the house? On the news you always hear about kids being beaten even after they were visited by social workers. Carmen probably would have thought Irma had been the one who called. She might have beaten her more severely to keep her quiet.

I never trusted anyone. That's why I didn't call. I thought it would just make the situation worse. Why should the adults at the hotlines be any different from the ones on my block? If the people in our building who knew Irma didn't do anything to help her, then what reason did I have to think total strangers would?

When something like this is happening around us and we keep silent, we're all to blame—including me. People always say, "Mind your own business." But when someone is being abused upstairs or down the hall and you're a witness, that abuse becomes part of your life as well. In other words, it *is* your business.

Silence isn't always golden. Sometimes silence is pain.

ANA ANGÉLICA PINES wrote this story when she was seventeen. She later attended New York University, majoring in film and television.

For more about where Ana is now, see page 169.

THINK ABOUT IT

- When is "minding your own business" the wrong thing to do? When is it the right thing?
- Have you ever felt torn between wanting to do the right thing and being afraid of getting involved? What choice did you make? Were you happy with your choice?

I WAS A CYBERBULLY

by Otis Hampton

When I was little, I was too afraid to speak up for myself. If I accidentally broke something, either my mom or my older brother would yell at me to tell the truth. When I tried to explain what happened, they'd tell me, "Shut up" or "Watch your mouth." They'd also hit me with their hands, belts, and other objects. I did as I was told, but inside I was angry.

It wasn't fair how sometimes I was beaten up for things that weren't my fault. Many times I wanted to tell my mom and brother that I hated them and that I wished they were dead, but fear of physical abuse prevented me from saying these things.

To make matters worse, I was also getting beaten up at school, partly because I have cerebral palsy and walk with a limp. Middle school was the worst. A lot of anger built up inside me.

In my freshman year of high school, I decided I wouldn't be silent anymore. One day, a group of us who knew each other from middle school were sitting at a table in the cafeteria, joking and throwing around insults. A kid I'll call Harry made a crack about my limp, and all the other kids started laughing. So I pointed out that he was missing several teeth and added, "hole-y sh—!"

"I decided I wouldn't be silent anymore."

The other kids at the table laughed, but Harry wrapped his hands around my throat and choked me. I looked into his eyes and I smiled an evil smile. I endured the pain and fear because I knew at some point Harry would let go.

After he did, I laughed, and everybody in the cafeteria looked at me like I was crazy. Laughing about being choked gave me a "never-say-die" persona. I began to present myself as fearless and outspoken, someone who wouldn't take anyone's nonsense.

I would throw insults like punches, and I got into a lot of verbal sparring. I never showed that people's disses hurt my feelings, but the "cripple" jokes did hurt. Ignorant high school freshmen would ask "What's wrong with you?" as if I were a freak. How could I explain why I walked with a limp?

If people tried to bully or belittle me, I'd go in for the kill. My weapons ranged from the classic "Yo Momma" jokes to personal attacks about their performance in school or their weight or race. I wanted to make them feel the same way they were making me feel.

My favorite thing to pick on was people's speech. Once a kid said to me, "Yo, yous a ugly n—, son. My dog look better den you," then laughed. I pretended to laugh with him for a few seconds and then said, "Maybe, but I bet your dog is smarter than you. I guess proper English isn't your thing." It seemed like my comments struck a nerve because he threatened to beat me up.

"I became an online bully."

Sometimes I stuck up for other kids, and that made me feel righteous. I told myself I was just being honest when I said mean things. But what was really going on, usually, was that I wanted my insults to hit close to the chest and hurt. I wasn't protecting others; I was behaving like a bully.

In ninth grade, I discovered the internet. My social life changed from that point on. People were judged more by their words and intelligence than by their appearance, physical strength, or personality. Since I have a good vocabulary and am a good writer, I suddenly had an advantage.

I tried out my "never-say-die" persona on websites like Facebook and YouTube. Insults flew freely in these places, and I joined the fray. After years of getting picked on, I attacked with rants and insults. I became an online bully. Physically I was safe in an internet fight. I could lash out at someone I didn't know—it's not like the person could reach through my computer screen and grab me by the throat.

No one was safe from my verbal assault, not even the friends I had online if they struck a nerve. My arrogance level went through the roof because there were no consequences when I bullied people online. I didn't consider anyone's feelings. Until one day, I lashed out at my mom on social media—and the consequences arrived in the real world.

I was furious at my mom for saying bad things about me to her friends. I got so mad that I posted a status update where I called my mom a b— and threatened to "burn the house down and smile about it." Now I can see the irony of the situation: I was doing what my mom had done to me—humiliating and threatening her in public. But at the time all I could see was my rage.

My aunt saw the post and called the cops. I wasn't there when they came to our house, but my mom was. When I heard the cops had shown up, I thought my mom would chew me up and spit me out when I got home. But surprisingly she seemed calm about the whole thing. She started by asking me, "Why would you say something like that? I love you and I'm good to you. I did not deserve that." She told me that what I said in that post hurt her.

I felt her pain. She was humiliated in public without actually being in public. I told her why I wrote the post—that I was upset about what she said about me. Then I apologized. We didn't talk much that night because we were both cooling down.

I had been bullied by my mom, my older brother, and kids at school. Now I realized that I had become a bully too. I felt terrible. My anger had brought my mom to tears. I realized that I used to write all those angry thoughts in my journal, but now I'd let them out where they could hurt people.

Just because you can't see the people you're threatening or insulting online doesn't mean you don't hurt them. If it goes out on the internet, that's bullying too.

OTIS HAMPTON was twenty when he wrote this story. After graduating from high school, Otis joined the Job Corps and was trained in medical administration.

THINK ABOUT IT

- Think of a time when you lashed out at someone who hurt you. Did you feel justified? Why or why not? Would you rather be silent and drop your anger, or would you try to talk to the person who hurt you? Why?
- Think of a time when you felt guilty about something you did or said to someone, thought of apologizing, and didn't. What stopped you? Was there a time when you thought you should apologize and did? Why did you apologize in that situation? How did it feel to apologize?

SOLDIER GIRL

by Max Morán

Once upon a time, not too long ago, while walking through a park I saw a pretty girl crying. So I stopped to ask her what was wrong. Little did I know she was going to be my best friend for months to come.

That day I took her for some ice cream and then for a hamburger. Funny thing was that we hung out all day without me knowing her name. She finally told me her name was Linda. She gave me her number that night, although I didn't even ask for it.

We hung out after that from time to time and had so much fun. But whenever I went over to her house, I got this feeling there was something wrong with her. The phone never rang for Linda, and I wondered why. She was such a cutie. Such a beautiful sight to see.

"All of a sudden my life didn't matter to me anymore. I was too concerned about Linda. She needed love so bad, so I decided to give her some of mine."

Linda had the most beautiful blue eyes I have ever seen. They looked just like the ocean. Her skin was so smooth—her whole body was brown sugar. I swear, if I had a kingdom, she would have been my Puerto Rican queen.

Whenever we spent time together, I'd have new suspicions about her. Linda was always tired and went to the doctor a lot. I felt when the time was right she would tell me what was wrong, and that's exactly what happened.

One night, she told me her secret. We were hugging each other when she pushed me away and said, "Max, I'm HIV-positive!" She looked at me and yelled, "Aren't you going to run and get out of my life like the rest?"

I smiled at her, hugged her, and gave her a kiss. I promised I would always be there for her, and that one day I'd give her the world. And if I couldn't, I was going to die trying. All of a sudden my life didn't matter to me anymore. I was too concerned about Linda. She needed love so bad, so I decided to give her some of mine.

She told me she got the disease from a friend who raped her, and now he was behind bars. She told me how hard it was for her to wake up every morning with no strength in her body. She was living with a disease that was stronger than her body, but not her mind. She never felt her life was over. She even had time to comfort me when I couldn't deal with my own life anymore.

"Her parents didn't give her much support. They were never around, and neither were her friends. So I did the best I could."

Sometimes when I looked sad, Linda knew what to do to make me feel better. She sat on my lap and picked my head up, while running her hands through my hair. Then she would say, "You're not ugly! You're so cute! Too handsome! If we weren't so young, I would marry you."

Then she would kiss me on my cheek and say, "You go, boy!" That was enough to put a smile on my face. Even though it was an innocent kiss, I felt butterflies in my stomach.

When Linda held my hand, I melted on the inside. Every time I got close to her, I got so nervous. I always felt nervous when I got close to a girl. Sometimes I felt anger and hatred when I thought about a guy taking advantage of such a beautiful person.

It must have been hard for Linda to think about her first and only intimate experience, because it was such a cruel one. She never asked me to make love to her. She wasn't selfish enough to ask me.

The truth is, I probably would have done it. I would have died for her. Her parents didn't give her much support. They were never around, and neither were her friends. So I did the best I could.

Our relationship grew to the point where she started wearing my clothes. She especially loved to wear my white and gray Army suit. So I decided to give it to her. That was the least I could do for her.

Linda trusted me so much that she invited me along when it was time for her to see the doctor. In many ways, she was more than a friend. She was two years older than me, so I guess she was like my older sister.

I loved her so much, and she knew how I felt, but we left it at that. We couldn't mess up a beautiful thing, although we kissed from time to time because we both needed the affection.

I knew Linda wasn't telling me the whole truth when she said she was HIV-positive. I knew she had full-blown AIDS. Still, I was by her side when her friends wouldn't dare to get within talking distance. I really don't know why people have to be so ignorant.

Whenever I could afford it, I bought Linda teddy bears and stuff like that. I was dying inside. I remember one of the last times we were together. It was at the park where we met. She asked me to take a walk near the lake with her. Once we got there, she pulled out a piece of paper and wrote these words on it: "Max and Linda. Friends forever."

Then she put the note inside a bottle and asked me to throw it as far as I could into the lake. We watched the bottle disappear from view.

That night we pledged our eternal friendship. We were like two fallen soldiers with tears rolling down from our eyes. She fell asleep by my side and had her head on my shoulder. I lay there for nearly an hour, feeling the late summer breeze cooling my body while it froze both of us in time. Then I picked Linda up and carried her home.

"I carried her just like a man would have carried a wounded soldier. My sweetheart was a soldier, but she was running out of time."

It was a long way from the park to her house. Ten blocks, which seemed like an eternity. With each step I took, it seemed that a piece of my heart was breaking. I felt that we were taking a walk from which neither of us would be returning. She didn't weigh much by now. Her heart weighed more than the two of us combined.

I carried her just like a man would have carried a wounded soldier. My sweetheart was a soldier, but she was running out of time. I got so mad whenever someone on the street looked at us in a strange way that I'd say to them, "What the hell are you looking at?"

Once we got to Linda's house, I laid her on the sofa. I went to her room and got a pillow and placed it under her head. Then I got a blanket and covered her entire body with it. All I kept thinking about was what I could do to put a smile on her pretty face.

She looked so cute that day wearing my oversized white and gray Army suit. My little soldier girl was fighting her own never-ending war. Linda was strong, so she fought hard to survive, but at the end her body gave up on us.

Within two months she was in the hospital, and it took a while for me to see her. When I finally got the chance, Linda didn't even have the energy to speak. But I understood what she wanted to say. So I got close to her and started singing her favorite song, "My Girl."

She smiled at me. All I could do was hold her hand. She kept looking at me while her eyes were closing with each passing second. When I was done singing, I kissed her one last time and put my forehead on top of her big heart.

There she was in a deep sleep; there she was on a stairway to heaven. There I was with a broken heart. There she was dreaming, maybe about the great times we had, the times when we wanted to save the world or when we proposed to each other. We always said yes. We'd planned to have two children, a boy and a girl. Our boy was supposed to grow up to be a baseball player, and our girl was going to sing sweeter songs than the birds up in the trees.

Now all those dreams were shattered. There was my fallen soldier on a long journey, hugging the teddy bear and the stuffed cat I had brought her. Good-bye, honey, I'll see you again someday.

I just didn't want her to leave me. I guess heaven must be a better place for my baby. That's where she belongs. It's too bad, because I'm never going to see her again. I cried so much for her. It's always the good ones who have to die.

Her parents never told me where her final resting place was, so I'll never be able to sing her favorite song to her again. Yet she knows that her final resting place is right here in my heart.

Even though I have now met someone I can truly say I love as much as Linda, sometimes I think that when Linda went to heaven, God took away my partner for life.

Rest in peace, honey. Oh, my soldier girl! I won't be true to you, but I will never forget you. I can't be true, because I must continue looking for my princess. You always told me to look for her.

It took me a while to get the courage to visit the park where Linda and I had spent so many good times together. One night I went to our spot deep in the woods, wondering how to talk to an angel. So I lay on the grass and started looking at the stars. Linda was the brightest one, and I had so many questions for her.

"Rest in peace, honey. Oh, my soldier girl!"

So, baby, how does it feel to be an angel? Am I headed up there soon? Do you still love me? Tell Elvis I said, "What's up?"

Days later I brought my Army suit with me and buried it in the middle of our spot. Months later I dug in the ground to see if the suit was still there, but it was gone. I wonder who took it. Maybe that place was another couple's spot too.

I would like to believe that Linda came down from heaven and took it. If not, there's someone, somewhere, wearing her favorite outfit. Who took it? Who?

MAX MORÁN was nineteen when he wrote this story. He came to the US from Honduras when he was ten, went into foster care when he was fifteen, and later lived on his own while pursuing a degree in social work.

For more about where Max is now, see page 169.

THINK ABOUT IT

- Think of when someone close to you was going through a painful time. Were you able to be there for the person? Or was it hard to share the pain?
- Have you ever had a close friendship—but not a romantic relationship—with someone of the opposite sex? If so, how did you feel about the relationship? If not, would you like to have a friendship like that?

HOW I MADE PEACE WITH THE PAST

by Paula Byrd

I remember the sadness in my mother's eyes as we sat in her hospital room, watching her deteriorate as the days went by. She had been in and out of the hospital for months, due to her illness and her misuse of drugs. My mother had AIDS, the disease that affects your immune system.

My youngest brother, Tyrone, and I had not been able to see her at first. My mother had to have an operation. We couldn't see her until she was able to speak.

But as soon as she was better, we went to see her. As we walked to her room, all of a sudden my heart just started beating real heavy. I thought it was going to stop right there. I was so scared, because I didn't know what to expect.

I had heard from my oldest brother, William, that she was getting worse. We finally went in, and as I got closer and closer to her bed, tears just started rolling down my face. I couldn't believe this small woman lying in the bed was my mother.

"My mother had AIDS, the disease that affects your immune system."

She had lost way too much weight. I wanted to hug her but was afraid of hurting her, so I didn't. I just said hello. You could hear in her voice that she was very sick and weak. It seemed as if she knew her time was coming.

She had gotten so sick that she wasn't able to move or get out of bed. She couldn't use the bathroom, so she was put in diapers. I didn't like the sight of my mother lying in bed powerless, unable to function. I tried to have a conversation with her.

"Hi, Ma. Are you all right? Is the hospital treating you good? Are you eating all your food?" (She didn't like the hospital food, so my brother brought her other food whenever he could.)

But her only reply was, "Yes, ma'am." From that day forward, our names became "ma'am."

You see, while my mother was in the hospital, the doctors found out she had a disease called dementia. (This is a loss of mental faculties. It's similar to Alzheimer's disease that older people get.)

While William was explaining her sickness to Tyrone and me, a tall lady entered the room. She introduced herself as Ms. Cynthia Allen, my mother's social worker. She started telling us how important it was that we come as often as we could, because no one knew when my mother was going to leave this earth.

I wanted to scream as loud as I could to get out all the anger I was feeling. It was my first time seeing her since she went into the hospital. I felt so confused when I tried to picture life without my mother. I knew it would be hard, because it would mean I wouldn't have a mother *or* a father.

> **"There was a time when I was so mad at my mother for not being there for us that I stopped going on home visits and kept myself isolated from her."**

I lost my father to AIDS and drugs also. Our mother was all we had, and soon we would have to give her up too. It was just too much to take in. But the most difficult thing I had to deal with as a female was that I wouldn't have a mother anymore.

I remembered all those times I would cry myself to sleep, because I missed her very much and I knew she was going to die. But I always thought the people who did research on AIDS would soon find a cure.

It was hurtful to know that soon she would no longer be there for me, because we were just beginning to build up our relationship again. My brothers and I had to grow up fast. We also have a new addition to our family, a five-year-old sister. She's also suffering with AIDS.

My sister was infected in the womb because my mother had unprotected sex. When my mother first found out that my sister had the disease, she gave her up for adoption. My sister is very well aware of her sickness, she's very healthy, and she takes her own medication daily.

There was a time when I was so mad at my mother for not being there for us that I stopped going on home visits and kept myself isolated from her. I was very bitter that she transmitted AIDS to my sister in the womb. I kept remembering her telling me how important it was never to have sex without a condom, because you could catch a disease. Then she went and did the opposite.

But after she went in the hospital, my thinking started to change. I had to learn to forgive her mistakes and accept what happened to her and my sister. It was a terrible mistake that my mother wouldn't have made had she not been taken over by drugs.

"I told her I knew she was sorry, but I couldn't hold in my anger toward her anymore. Expressing my feelings toward her enabled me to have faith in my mother again."

Her one-night stand for money cost my mother her kids, her health, and even her life. But what was done was now over. I had to overcome all that and learn to communicate with her. After all, she was still my mother, no matter what.

So slowly I began to build up a relationship with her. However, my first step in doing that was to let her know how she hurt me. I had to express my anger to her for the first time. She had done the one thing no child should ever have to face. She chose her boyfriend over her own children. I explained to her that she was wrong. She was my mother, and no man should come between us.

Her only reply was that she was sorry for everything she did. I also told her that I hated all her stealing and lying for money. I told her she should have been there for her children. A mother is supposed to help you, not hurt you.

She told me if she could take everything back she would, but she couldn't. She said she was truly sorry she had let her children down, but she would like to own up to her mistakes.

I told her I knew she was sorry, but I couldn't hold in my anger toward her anymore. Expressing my feelings toward her enabled me to have faith in my mother again.

I will never forget the day I went to the hospital to see her by myself. By then she had completely lost all her functions. She was unable to open her eyes or speak. But somehow my mother knew I was there, because she shook her head in response to what I was saying to her. I told her that I loved her and that I forgave her.

I also knew that deep down in her heart, she was sorry for everything she did in the past to my brothers and me. All was forgiven, and all grudges were put to rest. I also told her that I would make something of myself, no matter what, and that we as a family would always stick together.

Those were the last words I ever got to say to my mother. Soon after that, she died. Although she's passed on, I feel a part of her lives on in my little sister.

My sister is well aware of what's going on. She's very smart for her age. I know there will come a time when my sister will pass on, too, but for now I take one day at a time.

"I strongly advise kids who are going through what I have overcome to know the importance of letting your feelings out."

I accept all the negative things that have happened and focus on the positive. For instance, I want to make a better life for my brothers and me. I spend as much time with my sister as I can. Don't get me wrong—I miss my parents very dearly. But I try to think only about the good times, because that helps me cope better.

I put my faith in God. I pray that He will stand guard over my family and protect us from the negative influences out in the streets.

I strongly advise kids who are going through what I have overcome to know the importance of letting your feelings out. Once that person is gone, they're not coming back. If there's something you need to say, say it, even if the person hates the truth.

A lot of times you might feel that what happened to you is all right. You may feel you shouldn't say anything, because the person who committed the acts has suffered enough. Even if that's true, though, it's also important to let the person know it wasn't all right and they hurt you. Even though you forgive them, you should get your anger off your chest. It's important to let the person know how you feel, so that when they do pass on, you won't feel cheated.

As for my family and me, my mother got a chance to hear we loved her. It wasn't because of guilt, or because we knew she was going to die. It just was something we needed to say to her.

My point is, my mother got to hear how we felt about the whole situation before she was put to rest.

I wrote a poem that I'm sure everyone can relate to:

A Frozen Mind
The shock of a sudden death
Makes some people feel
As if their minds are frozen.
This may be nature's way
Of protecting your mind,
So that everything can sink in
Slowly, and you won't be
Overwhelmed.
But if you talk to others and
Share your sadness,
Your mind will slowly begin to
defrost,
and you will start to adjust to your
loss.
Love Always, Paula

PAULA BYRD was eighteen when she wrote this story. She lived in foster care for over eight years. She later received a college scholarship. "I will never forget what the foster care system has done for me," Paula says, "and the lessons I learned in the process."

For more about where Paula is now, see page 169.

THINK ABOUT IT

- Is there someone you're angry with, but haven't told about your anger? Why haven't you told the person? Is it hard to reveal your true feelings to him or her? What would you gain by expressing the anger? What would you lose?
- Is there someone in your life whom you have mixed feelings about—maybe both love and anger? How do you cope with your mixed feelings toward this person?

THE SEVEN RESILIENCIES

A SUMMARY

INSIGHT

ASKING TOUGH QUESTIONS

Insight is asking tough questions and giving honest answers about yourself and the difficult situations you find yourself in.

The opposite of **insight** is avoiding a painful truth.

Insight is hard because the urge to blame others for your troubles, instead of looking honestly at your own role, is powerful.

Insight helps you see things as they really are, not as you wish they would be.

INDEPENDENCE

BEING YOUR OWN PERSON

Independence is being your own person and keeping an emotional distance between you and the pressures of family, friends, and circumstances.

The opposite of **independence** is doing things only to get the approval of others or to avoid feeling alone or rejected.

Independence is hard because it sometimes means breaking or limiting connections with people who are important to you.

Independence helps you to feel safe and to know you can rely on yourself.

RELATIONSHIPS

CONNECTING WITH PEOPLE WHO MATTER

Relationships are connections with other people based on sharing, mutual respect, and openness.

The opposite of building **relationships** is cutting yourself off from others, protecting yourself by hiding behind a false front, or valuing other people only for what they can do for you.

Relationships are hard because you must give of yourself as well as take. **Relationships** require you to take risks and trust others.

Relationships give you understanding, friendship, and sometimes even love.

INITIATIVE

TAKING CHARGE

Initiative is taking action, meeting challenges, solving problems.

The opposite of taking **initiative** is giving up or feeling helpless.

Taking **initiative** is hard because some problems seem too overwhelming to solve.

Initiative helps you see that you can make a difference in your own life.

CREATIVITY

USING IMAGINATION

Creativity is using your imagination to express yourself and to handle hurt feelings and difficult experiences.

The opposite of **creativity** is keeping your feelings bottled up inside.

Creativity is hard because hurt feelings and painful experiences can weigh you down, dull your mind, and block your imagination.

Creativity helps you turn something that feels ugly and bad into something beautiful. **Creativity** helps you express your feelings in a positive, satisfying way.

HUMOR

FINDING WHAT'S FUNNY

Humor is finding what's funny, even when you're sad or in pain.

The opposite of **humor** is taking yourself and your situation too seriously.

Humor is hard because pressures can blot out the lighter side of life.

Humor helps you put pain in perspective. **Humor** helps you laugh and let others laugh with you.

MORALITY

DOING THE RIGHT THING

Morality is thinking of others as well as yourself. It's learning what other people need and trying to give it to them.

The opposite of **morality** is thinking only of yourself, or doing whatever suits you or whatever you can get away with.

Morality is hard because it can mean sacrificing your own best or short-term interests to do what's right for other people.

Morality helps connect you to other people through being useful and caring. **Morality** helps you feel you're a good person.

ABOUT YOUTH COMMUNICATION

Youth Communication equips and empowers educators and youth workers with real teen-written stories and a literacy-rich training model to engage struggling youth and build their social and emotional learning skills. Since 1980, Youth Communication's editorial staff has helped thousands of marginalized teens find their voices and write powerful, transformative stories. Educators and youth workers rely on these stories, and accompanying curricula and training, to connect with the youth they serve and to transform classrooms into dynamic, encouraging learning environments.

Youth Communication reaches educators with its stories and lessons through in-person and online professional development and coaching and through its curriculum programs and anthologies. Youth Communication also reaches educators (and teens) through various teen-written print and digital outlets, including ***YC****teen*, a general interest teen magazine (ycteenmag.org), and *Represent*, which focuses on stories about foster care and related issues (representmag.org).

Many young people who were first published by Youth Communication have become professional writers, including the novelist and MacArthur Fellow Edwidge Danticat; the prolific author and journalist Veronica Chambers; novelists Ernesto Quiñonez, Lucas Mann, and James Earl Hardy; novelist/screenwriter Kathy Ebel; journalists (and now journalism professors) Rachel Swarns and Mohamad Bazzi; essayist and author Sharon Feder; and poets Sheila Maldonado and Willie Perdomo.

Hundreds more Youth Communication alumni have made their marks in other fields. Ronald K. Brown is one of America's most significant choreographers and is known for the narrative quality of his dances. Shawn Dove founded and leads the Campaign for Black Male Achievement. Jamal Greene is a law professor at Columbia University, after working as a sports journalist and clerking for former US Supreme Court Justice John Paul Stevens. Gina Trapani created the Lifehacker website.

Countless other alumni work in teaching, social work, law, film, entertainment, tech, digital media, public relations, and other fields, where they use the storytelling skills they learned at Youth Communication to make a difference in their communities and the world.

For many of those alumni, one of the most gratifying aspects of their experience at Youth Communication is that years and even decades later, their stories are still being used to inform and inspire today's teens.

Youth Communication has won numerous awards for its books and curricula from the Association of American Publishers, the President's Committee on the Arts and the Humanities, and others.

For more information about Youth Communication's resources and professional development offerings, go to youthcomm.org.

ABOUT PROJECT RESILIENCE

Project Resilience, a private initiative located in Washington, D.C., was launched by Sybil Wolin, Ph.D., a developmental psychologist and educator, and Steven Wolin, M.D., a psychiatrist and researcher. The Wolins' interests converged when researchers, who had become disenchanted with vast literature on deficits in childhood studies, began to publish work on resilience in young people exposed to hardship. This offered an opportunity for change in settings where young people were viewed through the lens of a deficit bias.

From 1987 to 2000, Project Resilience provided training, consultation, and resources to clinics, schools, and agencies serving young people exposed to hardship. Its mission was to make resilience research accessible and to promote its application in services and policies for young people faced by adversity. Its work was facilitated by *The Resilient Self: How Survivors of Troubled Families Rise Above Adversity* by Sybil Wolin and Steven Wolin. *The Resilient Self* provided language and three essential concepts that rooted Project Resilience's practice in resilience research: the damage mindset, the challenge mindset, and the seven resiliencies.

In the damage mindset, young people are vulnerable and without resources to protect themselves. Hardship is like a toxic agent that infects them and causes deficits and disorders. Young people who are exposed to hardship are considered "at risk" and typically succumb to some form of pathology. Professionals with a damage mindset are on the lookout for problems that require the attention of experts whose tools are diagnosis, labels, and treatment. The damage mindset is a pessimistic view that drains the confidence of young people facing hardship and overlooks their struggle to endure.

In the challenge mindset, all young people are seen as having strengths. They are wired to be resilient, but they are not invincible. Hardship can be a destructive force that impedes their social and emotional development, learning, and adaptative behavior.

It can also challenge them to draw on their strengths and devise strategies for managing the hardships life has dealt them. The challenge mindset understands the interplay of vulnerabilities and resilience in young people exposed to hardship. It sees the harm that hardship can cause, but it chooses to foster strength rather than focus on problems. It is an optimistic view that energizes professionals and motivates young people to persist. When viewed through the lens of a challenge mindset, the true teen-written stories in *The Struggle to Be Strong* showcase the resilience these authors unconsciously reveal as they narrate the pain and difficulties of their lives.

Resiliencies are strengths mobilized by young people as they struggle with hardship. The seven resiliencies are meant to assist professionals in identifying and talking to young people challenged by hardship. Naming strengths conveys respect and honors the strategies young people devise to help themselves. It can change the self-image of those who have been identified by their problems, encouraging them to strive to improve their lives. The seven resiliencies—insight, independence, relationships, initiative, creativity, humor, and morality—were drawn from interviews the Wolins conducted with adults who had been burdened by hardship as children and who were currently solid people. They are the organizing framework for *The Struggle to Be Strong* and *A Leader's Guide to The Struggle to be Strong.*

ABOUT THE CONTRIBUTORS

Each story in *The Struggle to Be Strong* ends with information about where the author was shortly after the events of the story. In some cases, we have lost contact with the writers. But when possible, we have included below updated information about where writers are now and what they are doing.

Ana Angélica Pines graduated from New York University with a degree in film and television. She later earned an MBA from Baker College for Graduate Studies and worked as an online advocacy manager for Planned Parenthood of Northern California.

Angi Baptiste worked in retail after graduating from high school.

Artiqua S. Steed earned her associate's degree in business administration and a certification in business administration billing. She works in medical billing.

Chris Kanarick became a publicist for television, film, and plays.

Christopher A. Bogle graduated from Long Island University and later earned an M.A. in criminal justice from the John Jay College of Criminal Justice at the City University of New York.

Danny Gong earned a degree in sign language interpreting from LaGuardia Community College and an B.F.A. in dramatic writing from the Purchase College at the State University of New York. He became an interpreter for sign languages from American Sign Language to Japanese Sign Language.

Jamal K. Greene clerked for former US Supreme Court Justice John Paul Stevens. Jamal is now the Dwight Professor of Law at Columbia Law School.

Jamel A. Salter earned a B.S. in business and a master's degree in accounting. He now works as a real estate agent. He is also a pastor.

Max Morán earned an M.S.W. from the Silberman School of Social Work at Hunter College and became a school social worker.

Paula Byrd earned an associate's degree from Davidson Community College in North Carolina.

Shaniqua Sockwell worked in retail after graduating from high school.

Tamecka Crawford is a nutrition manager for an elementary school. She was named Georgia Manager of the Year in 2017.

Tonya Leslie earned a Ph.D. in education from New York University. She worked as an editor and vice president of professional learning at Scholastic.

Xavier Reyes earned a B.A. in public affairs from the Baruch College at the City University of New York and an M.S. in business management and leadership from the CUNY School of Professional Studies. He also taught high school.

GLOSSARY

boo: boyfriend

cracker: an insulting term for a white person

dogging: making fun of

foster care: a system in which minors, for a period of time, are cared for by people who are not their parents; also known as "the system"

foster family: the people who care for young people in the foster care system; these may be relatives of the child or people the child doesn't know

foster home: a household in which a young person in the foster care system is placed for care

group home: a residence licensed and monitored by the state mainly for older foster kids

irony: saying the opposite of what you mean

mad: lots of; very

metaphor: comparison of two unlike things where one is used in place of the other to suggest a similarity between them, such as describing a girl as a flower

play: to fool someone

scoping out: checking out

transgender: related to or being a person whose gender identity differs from the sex the person was assigned at birth

the Village: Greenwich Village, a neighborhood in New York City

GUIDE TO TOPICS

ABOUT THE EDITORS

AL DESETTA, M.A., worked for Youth Communication from 1985 to 2002 and served as editor of the organization's three youth-written publications: *Spofford Voices*, a poetry journal written by inmates at the Spofford Juvenile Detention Center in New York City; *New Youth Connections (NYC)*; and *Foster Care Youth United (FCYU)*. During the 1990–1991 academic year, he was a Charles H. Revson Fellow on the Future of the City of New York at Columbia University. He lives in upstate New York where he works as a ghostwriter. Visit his website at aldesetta.com.

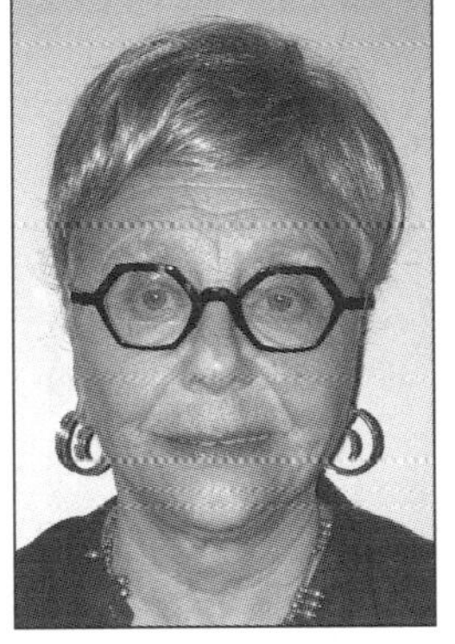

SYBIL WOLIN, PH.D., is a developmental psychologist. She was codirector of Project Resilience for over fifteen years and has been an advocate for children with special needs. She has taught high school English, adult education, and special education, and her writing has been published in many magazines and journals, including *Principal*, *Learning*, *Pediatric Clinics of North America*, *Resilience in Action*, and *Reaching Today's Youth*. In her retirement, Sybil has immersed herself in ancient Hebrew and in studying biblical writing through the lens of traditional commentary and contemporary literary analysis. After being an inveterate city dweller for her whole life, she now lives on the Chesapeake Bay with her husband.

Other Great Resources from Free Spirit

A Leader's Guide to The Struggle to Be Strong
How to Foster Resilience in Teens
by Sybil Wolin, Ph.D., Al Desetta, M.A., and Keith Hefner
(Updated Edition)
For teachers, youth workers, and other adults who work with teens in grades 7–12.
176 pp.; PB; 8½" x 11".

The Courage to Be Yourself
True Stories by Teens About Cliques, Conflicts, and Overcoming Peer Pressure
edited by Al Desetta, M.A., with Engaging Schools
For ages 13 & up.
160 pp.; PB; 6" x 9".

LGBTQ
The Survival Guide for Lesbian, Gay, Bisexual, Transgender, and Questioning Teens
(Revised & Updated 3rd Edition)
by Kelly Huegel Madrone
For ages 13 & up.
272 pp.; PB; two-color; 6" x 9".

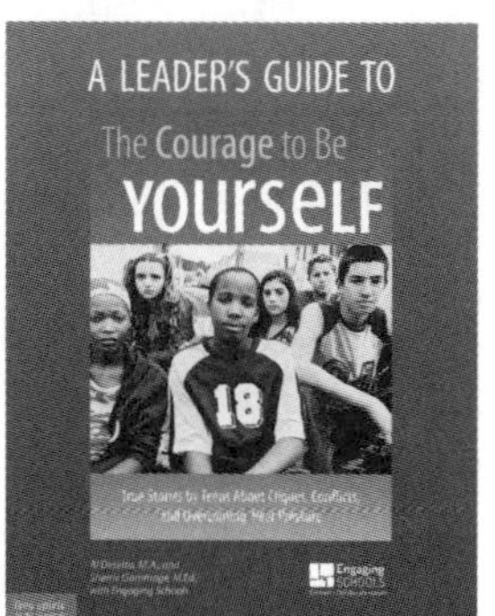

A Leader's Guide to The Courage to Be Yourself
by Al Desetta, M.A., with Engaging Schools
For youth workers, teachers, and leaders of teens in grades 7–12.
168 pp.; PB; 8½" x 11".

Interested in purchasing multiple quantities and receiving volume discounts? Contact edsales@freespirit.com or call 1.800.735.7323 and ask for Education Sales.

Many Free Spirit authors are available for speaking engagements, workshops, and keynotes. Contact speakers@freespirit.com or call 1.800.735.7323.

For pricing information, to place an order, or to request a free catalog, contact:

Free Spirit Publishing Inc.
6325 Sandburg Road • Suite 100 • Minneapolis, MN 55427-3674
toll-free 800.735.7323 • local 612.338.2068 • fax 612.337.5050
help4kids@freespirit.com • freespirit.com